FORGOTTEN VOICES

FORGOTTEN VOICES

Dissenting Southerners in an Age of Conformity

EDITED BY

CHARLES E. WYNES

LOUISIANA STATE UNIVERSITY PRESS

973.8
W985

To

LILLIAN SMITH

Courageous keeper of the Southern liberal tradition

The supreme question in the South is,
shall we be a free people
or shall we be the slaves of a vile partisanship?

JOHN CARLISLE KILGO, 1902

Contents

Illustrations

FORGOTTEN VOICES

Introduction

It has never been a popular course of action for white men in the South to stand up for the rights of Negroes. Indeed it often has been physically dangerous for them to do so, and, at all times, to do so has meant some degree of ostracism. Many have also found it expedient to leave the South once they have spoken out against "the Southern way of life."

At no time in the South's history has this been more true than in the period of roughly 1885-1917. Yet for several years following the end of Reconstruction there were what C. Vann Woodward has called "forgotten alternatives" to racism. These alternatives were practiced by white supremacy-minded Southern leaders who had overthrown the Carpetbag regimes and who accepted as part of the new Southern way of life segregation customs which had grown up during Reconstruction, or even before the Civil War. For all their condemnation of "Negro equality" during Reconstruction, these leaders—the so-called Redeemers—generally tended to accept the South, including the Negro, as they found it. Certainly, though they sought to curb his political power, or, better yet, to control that power for their interests, there was no determined drive to demean and debase the Negro and create a completely segregated society. That came later, beginning in the late 1880's and culminating, in most instances, at about the time the United States entered World War I. Meanwhile, under the Redeemers, the South was both segregated and integrated, just as was the case in the North. Inconsistency was thus the most distinguishing factor in the matter of Negro acceptance, rejection, or segregation on the common carriers and in many, if not most, public accommodations. In the newspapers, memoirs, and travel accounts of the day, for every instance one can find of Negroes being segregated, evicted, or refused service at some public facility, another instance can be found of unquestioned acceptance.

Then something happened, or, as Professor Woodward has written, the South capitulated to racism. The reasons why it did so are both simple and complex, and it might also be said that they are not wholly clear or generally agreed upon. Explanations run the gamut from abandonment of the Negro by the Republican party to change in the ideology of reform—from the old idealistic belief that man and society could be reformed by men to that of a Social Darwinian naturalism, in which the Negro and all men were left to rise or fall as a result of their own efforts and general fitness. Likewise there is the belief, held by Professor Woodward and some others, that the increase of Jim Crow laws "is almost an accurate index of the decline of the reactionary regimes of the Redeemers and triumph of white democratic movements"—certainly true in some Southern states but doubtful in others.

Then there are two other explanations—failure of the democratic agrarian revolt known as Populism, and national fear of extending democracy to the peoples who came to constitute America's share of the white man's burden. The Populist revolt had threatened the one-party hegemony of the Democrats, and in doing so further threatened to place the Negro in a position of holding the balance of power. Hence, after Populist failure it was argued that if white men were ever to divide in the South, the "threat" of the Negro must first be removed. Disfranchisement followed, together with further segregation. Meanwhile, as the nation acquired an island empire of brown-skinned peoples, the North agreed with the South that such people were neither fit for self-government nor for all the rights and privileges of American citizens. Such national attitudes created the perfect atmosphere for both disfranchisement and enforced segregation of the Negro in the South. Finally, there was Progressivism itself. Not only were virtually all the South's progressive political leaders white supremacists, they also sincerely believed that the only way to remove the bribery, vote buying, ballot box stuffing, etc., which had plagued the South since the Civil War, was to remove the Negro from the political scene altogether, so that white men would not have to cheat one another in an attempt to obtain the Negro's vote. Therefore it was easier, morally as well as politically, to segregate or further segregate a people who did not even have the ballot.

No one of the above reasons or explanations for disfranchisement and enforced segregation can alone explain why, after a generation of Negro voting during which there was practiced a most inconsistent policy of segregation, the ballot should then be taken away from the Negro, while the dignity of his manhood was demeaned by a system of rigid and state-enforced segregation. Together, though, all of the above reasons, here greatly abbreviated and simplified, serve to make up the best explanation that we have.

After the "deep freeze" set in, so far as a rational approach to race was concerned, there were still white Southerners who dissented from such a spirit of conformity. But there was never any great body of public opinion constituting the "Silent South," in which George Washington Cable, one of the "forgotten voices," placed his faith.

The ranks of these men were thin, as evidenced by the smallness of the present volume. But there is no way of knowing or judging how many there really were, since only the most literate left written record of their views. Also, only the most courageous, or economically and socially secure, dared to speak out in a vein bound to incur the censure of the majority. And having spoken, there were few, if any, to defend them, while the multitude either condemned, or perhaps worse, simply ignored them.

There follow seven such essays by seven forgotten voices. The editor does not mean to imply that these men, or at least some of them, are literally forgotten, and their liberal views wholly unknown today. Rather, the adjective "forgotten" is used only as Professor Woodward used it in his expression, "forgotten alternatives." Just as there were other routes which the South might have continued to follow in the tortured racial situation, so there were other Southern voices which the region might have heeded. It did not, of course, and more is the tragedy for all the nation.

George Washington Cable, author of the first essay, has never been forgotten as a novelist of Creole Louisiana. And as a result of the work of Arlin Turner, in a fine biography and in a collection of Cable's essays on the South and the Negro, the nation recently has been reminded that Cable was a discerning and foremost social critic of the South in the late last century. Bishop Thomas U. Dudley, author of the second essay, is generally unknown to even the educated reader, except one especially interested in the history of the Episcopal church. Tom Watson of Georgia is a very special case: he enjoys the distinction of being the only Southern political figure of this period to call upon the South to see the Negro as a man, not as a black man. Of course Watson's is not a forgotten voice, but it is remembered as a voice of racism, that of a hater of Negroes, Jews, and Catholics. Lewis Harvie Blair was wealthy enough to afford his generally radical views, but even so, his was an unknown and forgotten voice until given new life by recent scholarship. Andrew Sledd and John Spencer Bassett, especially the latter, certainly are well known and remembered in academic circles, as both men were involved in the issue of academic freedom as a result of their views on the race question. Quincy Ewing, the author of the last essay, will perhaps be known to the fewest number of readers of any of the seven authors represented here. His voice is not only forgotten, it is virtually unknown as well.

These, then, are the seven Southerners represented in this collection of heretical views on the race question. (More about each of them and their lives and writings will be found in the headnotes to each essay.) What, if anything, besides their humanitarian interests did they have in common? All of them were born in the South and all were of Southern parentage, except Cable, whose mother was from New England, but his father was a native of Virginia. The oldest of them, Blair, was born in 1834 and the youngest, Sledd, in 1870. Three were natives of Virginia—Blair, Sledd, and Dudley—but only Blair remained there and wrote from there. Two were natives of Louisiana—Cable and Ewing—and both were living there when they wrote the essays included here. Of the remaining two, Watson was born in Georgia and Bassett in North Carolina, while each wrote from his native state. All of them can be considered educated men. Dudley, Sledd, Bassett, and Ewing were college graduates; Watson had attended college for two years at Mercer in Macon and then gone on to become a leading lawyer in the state; Cable was wholly self-educated and Blair largely so. By profession three of the seven were ministers, Dudley and Ewing in the Episcopal church, and Sledd, who was also a teacher of Latin and theology, in the Methodist church. Bassett was a professor of history, Blair a wealthy businessman, and Watson a lawyer and politician. All, except Blair, who was fifty-nine when he wrote the essay included here, and Dudley, who was forty-eight, were young or relatively young men. Cable was forty-one, Watson thirty-six, Sledd thirty-two, Bassett thirty-six, and Ewing forty-two. Following appearance of their essays Dudley, Watson, Blair, Sledd, and Ewing all continued to live in the South. Sledd left briefly to complete his Ph.D. degree at Yale, while twenty years later Ewing accepted charge of a parish in California, but for only five years, after which he returned to the South. Except for Sledd, these five continued to live in the same locality and among neighbors, many if not most of whom they had offended. Three years after the "Bassett Affair," which erupted following Bassett's declaration that Booker T. Washington was the "greatest man, save General Lee, born in the South in a hundred years," Bassett left the South, but only because of greater professional opportunity elsewhere. Cable, alone, might be said to have been almost driven from his native land, though he, too, had good professional reasons for leaving. Without doubt, though, he was pilloried more than any of the others. Finally, of the seven, only Watson and Blair ever renounced their liberal views. The others apparently continued to hold to their liberal position on the race question. However, all, including Cable after 1892, did so less and less openly, wrote nothing further on the Negro, and concentrated upon other reforms.

It is impossible to give an unequivocal answer to the question of why Watson and Blair made a complete about-face on the race question. Neither man ever himself offered an explanation except for Blair's reported and coldly reasoned remark: "I think I [earlier] reasoned logically from my premises, but since then, experience and observation have convinced me of the fallacy of my premises." Men simply react differently to the same circumstances. While all of the authors discussed here apparently despaired of the fight for Negro rights and his general uplift, as witnessed by their own records, only Watson and Blair were so embittered as to strike out against the very people they had sought to help. For Watson, the Negro had been the "Nemesis" which had not only stymied his own political career on the national scene, but prevented success of any independent political movement in the South, in this case Populism. In fury and frustration he turned on the Negro as well as upon Catholics and Jews, literally in a paranoid manner. Blair is much more difficult to explain. Certainly his liberal views on Negro rights had not hampered him in amassing a fortune. Perhaps they did hurt him socially, in socially conscious Richmond, but Blair was a loner anyway, who at least outwardly cared nothing for a social life, preferring to devote all his energies to his business, his family, and reading. But with a businessman's hardheaded realism, he must have had little taste for continued devotion to even an ideal which after a dozen years was further from reality than when he had first championed it.

For while Watson stood to gain national office and prestige by embracing the climate of racism, there was no such reward for Blair. He had earlier wanted to see the Negro uplifted, with no door to opportunity barred to him, because to do so, he said, was the only way to uplift the whole South. Somehow, though, he lost all faith in the Negro's ability to rise, even if given the opportunity. So believing, he wrote that "the only thing to do is to elevate him . . . as a very different being—a negro . . . in line with his African nature and antecedents." Blair remained, however, an ardent and typical Southern Progressive—that is, he believed that Progressivism and its fruits were for whites only. Really, Blair's reversal of position defies explanation. I have been able to come up with no better explanation than the one which I offered several years ago: "In spite of all the inconsistencies and reversals of position in his life, Blair was true to two ideals—logic and rebellion against conformity. And he never allowed fidelity to the latter to lead him astray from logic, as witnessed by the repudiation of his earlier conclusions . . . because he became convinced that his initial premises had been wrong."

The essays which follow appeared over a period of nearly a quarter of a century, between 1885 and 1909. Hence, the racial situation from which Ewing dissented in 1909 was different from that about which Cable wrote in 1885. In 1885, though Negroes frequently met segregation, nowhere was it statewide and rigid. Not until 1887 was the first railroad segregation enacted, in Florida, and not until 1890 did the first state, Mississippi, disfranchise the Negro through a new constitution. In 1909, however, when Ewing wrote, all the Southern states had a myriad of segregation statutes, and all had provided for virtual disfranchisement of the Negro. In a word, when Cable, Dudley, Watson, and Blair wrote, there were still oft-followed alternatives to racism; while those who wrote after 1900, Sledd, Bassett, and Ewing, were dissenting from a rigid atmosphere of racist conformity. It was this situation, with few changes, which lasted into the decade of the 1950's. No wonder, by the first decade of the twentieth century, the earlier dissenters had already despaired, while the later ones soon ceased their efforts too.

Modern-day readers of these essays will find some of the liberalism more than a little dated, and will discover, here and there, now completely discredited beliefs about the natural ability and potential of Negro peoples. They should remember, however, that for the time and place in which they were written all were absolutely heretical. Occasionally, at least in certain passages, these essays are as fresh and timely today as they were when they were first written. They all stand as a vital part of the South's liberal heritage.

GEORGE WASHINGTON CABLE

When "The Freedman's Case in Equity" was first published in the *Century Magazine* in 1885, George Washington Cable was already one of the nation's best-known living novelists. In literary stature no other Southerner was even close to him. New Orleans, his native city and his home, certainly was proud to claim him. Yet, within a year this twice-wounded Confederate veteran and son of slave-owning parents found it expedient to move permanently from the South, to Northampton, Massachusetts. While other factors from both his personal and professional life entered into the decision to move, the vilification he had received at home following publication of "The Freedman's Case in Equity" was a powerful incentive to his leaving.

Declaring in the essay that "the greatest social problem before the American people today is, as it has been for a hundred years, the presence among us of the Negro," Cable commenced a decade of research, speaking, and writing on the Southern need for reform. He covered not only the Negro, but the more general areas of education, the crop lien system, taxes, distribution of wealth, Southern migration, and Southern constitutions and statutes. In spite of the abuse heaped upon him, he was convinced that there existed a "Silent South," a great body of public opinion which secretly agreed with him. In this conviction, he was unduly optimistic, but perhaps he needed to believe it in order to have the courage to carry on the fight.

In his first controversial essay on the Negro, Cable laid out the framework for his civil rights struggle of the coming years, and in it are to be found intimations of the themes yet to come from his pen. The Negro had been freed, but he was not a free man in a society thoroughly dominated by the white man. The convict lease system was bad, chiefly because it was directed against the Negro. And separate schools, like other separate accommodations, were bad because they stamped the badge of permanent, caste-like inferiority upon the Negro—in the name of prevention of social equality. A moralist, whereas Lewis Harvie Blair, a contemporary heretic, was a pragmatic realist, Cable concluded that it was no longer a question of "whether constitutional amendments, but whether the eternal principles of justice, are violated." Cable pleaded with the South not to demean, insult, and permanently degrade the Negro, because it was morally and ethically wrong to do so. Blair argued, practically but not without humane feeling, that it was simply too costly to the whole South to do so. Both were, of course, right.

The
Freedman's Case
in Equity

T HE greatest social problem before the American people today
is, as it has been for a hundred years, the presence among
us of the Negro.*

No comparable entanglement was ever drawn round itself by
any other modern nation with so serene a disregard of its ultimate
issue, or with a more distinct national responsibility. The African
slave was brought here by cruel force, and with everybody's consent except his own. Everywhere the practice was favored as a
measure of common aggrandizement. When a few men and
women protested, they were mobbed in the public interest, with
the public consent. There rests, therefore, a moral responsibility
on the whole nation never to lose sight of the results of African-
American slavery until they cease to work mischief and injustice.

It is true these responsibilities may not fall everywhere with the
same weight; but they are nowhere entirely removed. The original
seed of trouble was sown with the full knowledge and consent
of the nation. The nation was to blame; and so long as evils
spring from it, their correction must be the nation's duty.

The late Southern slave has within two decades risen from
slavery to freedom, from freedom to citizenship, passed on into
political ascendency, and fallen again from that eminence. The
amended Constitution holds him up in his new political rights as
well as a mere constitution can. On the other hand, certain
enactments of Congress, trying to reach further, have lately been
made void by the highest court of the nation. And another thing

*Reprinted from *Century Magazine*, XXIX (January, 1885), 409–18.

has happened. The popular mind in the old free states, weary of strife at arm's length, bewildered by its complications, vexed by many a blunder, eager to turn to the cure of other evils, and even tinctured by that race feeling whose grosser excesses it would so gladly see suppressed, has retreated from its uncomfortable dictational attitude and thrown the whole matter over to the states of the South. Here it rests, no longer a main party issue, but a group of questions which are to be settled by each of these states separately in the light of simple equity and morals, and which the genius of American government does not admit of being forced upon them from beyond their borders. Thus the whole question, become secondary in party contest, has yet reached a period of supreme importance.

Before slavery ever became a grave question in the nation's politics—when it seemed each state's private affair, developing unmolested—it had two different fates in two different parts of the country. In one, treated as a question of public equity, it withered away. In the other, overlooked in that aspect, it petrified and became the cornerstone of the whole social structure; and when men sought its overthrow as a national evil, it first brought war upon the land, and then grafted into the citizenship of one of the most intelligent nations in the world six millions of people from one of the most debased races on the globe.

And now this painful and wearisome question, sown in the African slave trade, reaped in our civil war, and garnered in the national adoption of millions of an inferior race, is drawing near a second seed time. For this is what the impatient proposal to make it a dead and buried issue really means. It means to recommit it to the silence and concealment of the covered furrow. Beyond that incubative retirement no suppressed moral question can be pushed; but all such questions, ignored in the domain of private morals, spring up and expand once more into questions of public equity; neglected as matters of public equity, they blossom into questions of national interest; and, despised in that guise, presently yield the red fruits of revolution.

This question must never again bear that fruit. There must arise, nay, there has arisen, in the South itself, a desire to see established the equities of the issue; to make it no longer a question of endurance between one group of states and another, but between the moral debris of an exploded evil and the duty, necessity, and value of planting society firmly upon universal justice and equity. This, and this only, can give the matter final burial. True, it is still a question between states; but only secondarily, as something formerly participated in, or as it concerns every householder to know that what is being built against his house is built by level and plummet. It is the interest of the Southern states first, and *consequently* of the whole land, to discover clearly these equities and the errors that are being committed against them.

If we take up this task, the difficulties of the situation are plain. We have, first, a revision of Southern state laws which has forced into them the recognition of certain human rights discordant with the sentiments of those who have always called themselves the community; second, the removal of the entire political machinery by which this forcing process was effected; and, third, these revisions left to be interpreted and applied under the domination of these antagonistic sentiments. These being the three terms of the problem, one of three things must result. There will arise a system of vicious evasions eventually ruinous to public and private morals and liberty, or there will be a candid reconsideration of the sentiments hostile to these enactments, or else there will be a division, some taking one course and some the other.

This is what we should look for from our knowledge of men and history; and this is what we find. The revised laws, only where they could not be evaded, have met that reluctant or simulated acceptance of their narrowest letter which might have been expected—a virtual suffocation of those principles of human equity which the unwelcome decrees do little more than shadow forth. But in different regions this attitude has been made in very different degrees of emphasis. In some the new principles have grown, or are growing, into the popular conviction, and the opposing sentiments are correspondingly dying out. There are even some limited districts where they have received much practical acceptance. While, again, other sections lean almost wholly toward the old sentiments; an easy choice, since it is the conservative, the unyielding attitude, whose strength is in the absence of intellectual and moral debate.

Now, what are the gains, what the losses of these diverse attitudes? Surely these are urgent questions to any one in our country who believes it is always a losing business to be in the wrong. Particularly in the South, where each step in this affair is an unprecedented experience, it will be folly if each region, small or large, does not study the experiences of all the rest. And yet this, alone, would be superficial; we would still need to do more. We need to go back to the roots of things and study closely, analytically, the origin, the present foundation, the rationality, the rightness, of those sentiments surviving in us which prompt an attitude qualifying in any way peculiarly the black man's liberty among us. Such a treatment will be less abundant in incident, less picturesque; but it will be more thorough.

First, then, what are these sentiments? Foremost among them stands the idea that he is of necessity an alien. He was brought to our shores a naked, brutish, unclean, captive, pagan savage, to be and remain a kind of connecting link between man and the beasts of burden. The great changes to result from his contact with a superb race of masters were not taken into account. As a social factor he was intended to be as purely zero as the brute at the other end of his plow line. The occasional mingling of his blood with that of the white man worked no change in the sentiment; one, two, four, eight, multiplied upon or divided into zero, still gave zero for the result. Generations of American nativity made no difference; his children and children's children were born in sight of our door, yet the old notion held fast. He increased to vast numbers, but it never wavered. He accepted our dress, language, religion, all the fundamentals of our civilization, and became forever expatriated from his own land; still he remained, to us, an alien. Our sentiment went blind. It did not see that gradually, here by force and there by choice, he was fulfilling a host of conditions that earned at least a solemn moral right to that naturalization which no one at first had dreamed of giving him. Frequently he even bought back the freedom of which he had been robbed, became a taxpayer, and at times an educator of his children at his own expense; but the old idea of alienism passed laws to banish him, his wife, and children by thousands from the state, and threw him into loathsome jails as a common felon for returning to his native land.

It will be wise to remember that these were the acts of an enlightened, God-fearing people, the great mass of whom have passed beyond all earthly accountability. They were our fathers. I am the son and grandson of slaveholders. These were their faults; posterity will discover ours; but these things must be frankly, fearlessly taken into account if we are ever to understand the true interests of our peculiar state of society.

Why, then, did this notion that the man of color must always remain an alien stand so unshaken? We may readily recall how, under ancient systems, he rose not only to high privileges, but often to public station and power. Singularly, with us the trouble lay in a modern principle of liberty. The whole idea of American government rested on all men's equal, inalienable right to secure their life, liberty, and the pursuit of happiness by governments founded in their own consent. Hence, our Southern forefathers, shedding their blood, or ready to shed it, for this principle, yet proposing in equal good conscience to continue holding the American black man and mulatto and quadroon in slavery, had to anchor that conscience, their conduct, and their laws in the conviction that the man of African tincture was, not by his master's arbitrary assertion merely, but by nature and unalterably, an alien. If that hold should break, one single wave of irresistible inference would lift our whole Southern social fabric and dash it upon the rocks of Negro emancipation and enfranchisement. How was it made secure? Not by books, though they were written

among us from every possible point of view, but, with the mass
of our slave-owners, by the calm hypothesis of a positive, intuitive
knowledge. To them the statement was an axiom. They abandoned
the methods of moral and intellectual reasoning, and fell back
upon this assumption of a God-given instinct, nobler than reason,
and which it was an insult to a freeman to ask him to prove on
logical grounds.

Yet it was found not enough. The slave multiplied. Slavery was
a dangerous institution. Few in the South today have any just
idea how often the slave plotted for his freedom. Our Southern
ancestors were a noble, manly people, springing from some of the
most highly intelligent, aspiring, upright, and refined nations of the
modern world; from the Huguenot, the French Chevalier, the Old
Englander, the New Englander. Their acts were not always right;
whose are? But for their peace of mind they had to believe them
so. They therefore spoke much of the Negro's contentment with
that servile condition for which nature had designed him. Yet
there was no escaping the knowledge that we dared not trust the
slave caste with any power that could be withheld from them. So
the perpetual alien was made also a perpetual menial, and the
belief became fixed that this, too, was nature's decree, not ours.

Thus we stood at the close of the Civil War. There were always
a few Southerners who did not justify slavery, and many who
cared nothing whether it was just or not. But what we have described was the general sentiment of good Southern people. There
was one modifying sentiment. It related to the slave's spiritual
interests. Thousands of pious masters and mistresses flatly broke
the shameful laws that stood between their slaves and the Bible.
Slavery was right; but religion, they held, was for the alien and
menial as well as for the citizen and master. They could be alien
and citizen, menial and master, in church as well as out; and they
were.

Yet over against this lay another root of today's difficulties. This
perpetuation of the alien, menial relation tended to perpetuate the
vices that naturally cling to servility, dense ignorance and a hope-

less separation from true liberty; and as we could not find it in our minds to blame slavery with this perpetuation, we could only assume as a further axiom that there was, by nature, a disqualifying moral taint in every drop of Negro blood. The testimony of an Irish, German, Italian, French, or Spanish beggar in a court of justice was taken on its merits; but the colored man's was excluded by law wherever it weighed against a white man. The colored man was a prejudged culprit. The discipline of the plantation required that the difference between master and slave be never lost sight of by either. It made our master caste a solid mass, and fixed a common masterhood and subserviency between the ruling and the serving race. Every one of us grew up in the idea that he had, by birth and race, certain broad powers of police over any and every person of color.

All at once the tempest of war snapped off at the ground every one of these arbitrary relations, without removing a single one of the sentiments in which they stood rooted. Then, to fortify the freedman in the tenure of his new rights, he was given the ballot. Before this grim fact the notion of alienism, had it been standing alone, might have given way. The idea that slavery was right did begin to crumble almost at once. "As for slavery," said an old Creole sugar-planter and former slaveowner to me, "it was damnable." The revelation came like a sudden burst of light. It is one of the South's noblest poets [Maurice Thompson] who has but just said:

> I am a Southerner;
> I love the South; I dared for her
> To fight from Lookout to the sea,
> With her proud banner over me:
> But from my lips thanksgiving broke,
> As God in battle-thunder spoke,
> And that Black Idol, breeding drouth
> And dearth of human sympathy
> Throughout the sweet and sensuous South,

Was, with its chains and human yoke,
Blown hellward from the cannon's mouth,
While Freedom cheered behind the smoke!

With like readiness might the old alien relation have given way if we could only, while letting that pass, have held fast by the other old ideas. But they were all bound together. See our embarrassment. For more than a hundred years we had made these sentiments the absolute essentials to our self-respect. And yet if we clung to them, how could we meet the freedman on equal terms in the political field? Even to lead would not compensate us; for the fundamental profession of American politics is that the leader is servant to his followers. It was too much. The ex-master and ex-slave—the quarter-deck and the forecastle, as it were—could not come together. But neither could the American mind tolerate a continuance of martial law. The agonies of reconstruction followed.

The vote, after all, was a secondary point, and the robbery and bribery on one side, and whipping and killing on the other, were but huge accidents of the situation. The two main questions were really these: on the freedman's side, how to establish republican state government under the same recognition of his rights that the rest of Christendom accorded him; and on the former master's side, how to get back to the old semblance of republican state government, and—allowing that the freedman was de facto a voter—still to maintain a purely arbitrary superiority of all whites over all blacks, and a purely arbitrary equality of all blacks among themselves as an alien, menial, and dangerous class.

Exceptionally here and there some one in the master caste did throw off the old and accept the new ideas, and, if he would allow it, was instantly claimed as a leader by the newly liberated thousands around him. But just as promptly the old master race branded him also an alien reprobate, and in ninety-nine cases out of a hundred, if he had not already done so, he soon began to confirm by his actions the brand on his cheek. However, we need give no history here of the dreadful episode of Reconstruction. Under an experimentative truce its issues rest today upon the pledge of the wiser leaders of the master class: Let us but remove the hireling demagogue, and we will see to it that the freedman is accorded a practical, complete, and cordial recognition of his equality with the white man before the law. As far as there has been any understanding at all, it is not that the originally desired ends of Reconstruction have been abandoned, but that the men of North and South have agreed upon a new, gentle, and peaceable method for reaching them; that, without change as to the ends in view, compulsory reconstruction has been set aside and a voluntary reconstruction is on trial.

It is the fashion to say we paused to let the "feelings engendered by the war" pass away, and that they are passing. But let not these truths lead us into error. The sentiments we have been analyzing, and upon which we saw the old compulsory reconstruction go hard aground—these are not the "feelings engendered by the war." We must disentangle them from the "feelings engendered by the war," and by Reconstruction. They are older than either. But for them slavery would have perished of itself, and emancipation and reconstruction been peaceful revolutions.

Indeed, as between master and slave, the "feelings engendered by the war" are too trivial, or at least were too short-lived, to demand our present notice. One relation and feeling the war destroyed: the patriarchal tie and its often really tender and benevolent sentiment of dependence and protection. When the slave became a freedman the sentiment of alienism became for the first time complete. The abandonment of this relation was not one-sided; the slave, even before the master, renounced it. Countless times, since reconstruction began, the master has tried, in what he believed to be everybody's interest, to play on that old sentiment. But he found it a harp without strings. The freedman could not formulate, but he could see, all our old ideas of autocracy and subserviency, of master and menial, of an arbitrarily fixed class to guide and rule, and another to be guided and ruled. He rejected the overture. The old master, his well-meant condescensions slighted, turned away estranged, and justified himself in passively withholding that simpler protection without patronage which any one American citizen, however exalted, owes to any other, however humble. Could the freedman in the bitterest of those days have consented to throw himself upon just that one old relation, he could have found a physical security for himself and his house such as could not, after years of effort, be given him by constitutional amendments, Congress, United States marshals, regiments of regulars, and ships of war. But he could not; the very nobility of the civilization that had held him in slavery had made him too much a man to go back to that shelter; and by his manly neglect to do so he has proved to us who once ruled over him that, be his relative standing among the races of men what it may, he is worthy to be free.

To be a free man is his still distant goal. Twice he has been a freedman. In the days of compulsory reconstruction he was freed in the presence of his master by that master's victorious foe. In these days of voluntary reconstruction he is virtually freed by the consent of his master, but the master retaining the exclusive right to define the bounds of his freedom. Many everywhere have taken up the idea that this state of affairs is the end to be desired and the end actually sought in reconstruction as handed over to the states. I do not charge such folly to the best intelligence of any American community; but I cannot ignore my own knowledge that the average thought of some regions rises to no better idea of the issue. The belief is all too common that the nation, having aimed at a wrong result and missed, has left us of the Southern states to get now such other result as we think best. I say this belief is not universal. There are those among us who see that America has no room for a state of society which makes its lower classes harmless by abridging their liberties, or, as one of the favored class lately said to me, has "got 'em so they don't give no trouble." There is a growing number who see that the one thing we cannot afford to tolerate at large is a class of people less than citizens; and that every interest in the land demands that the freedman be free to become in all things, as far as his own personal gifts will lift and sustain him, the same sort of American citizen he would be if, with the same intellectual and moral caliber, he were white.

Thus we reach the ultimate question of fact. Are the freedman's liberties suffering any real abridgment? The answer is easy. The letter of the laws, with but few exceptions, recognizes him as entitled to every right of an American citizen; and to some it may seem unimportant that there is scarcely one public relation of life in the South where he is not arbitrarily and unlawfully compelled to hold toward the white man the attitude of an alien, a menial, and a probable reprobate, by reason of his race and color. One of the marvels of future history will be that it was counted a small matter, by a majority of our nation, for six millions of people within it, made by its own decree a component part of it, to be subjected to a system of oppression so rank that nothing could make it seem small except the fact that they had already been ground under it for a century and a half.

Examine it. It proffers to the freedman a certain security of life and property, and then holds the respect of the community, that dearest of earthly boons, beyond his attainment. It gives him certain guarantees against thieves and robbers, and then holds him under the unearned contumely of the mass of good men and women. It acknowledges in constitutions and statutes his title to an American's freedom and aspirations, and then in daily practice heaps upon him in every public place the most odious distinctions, without giving ear to the humblest plea concerning mental or moral character. It spurns his ambition, tramples upon his languishing self-respect, and indignantly refuses to let him either buy with money, or earn by any excellence of inner life or outward behavior, the most momentary immunity from these public indignities even for his wife and daughters. Need we cram these pages with facts in evidence, as if these were charges denied and requiring to be proven? They are simply the present avowed and defended state of affairs peeled of its exteriors.

Nothing but the habit, generations old, of enduring it could make it endurable by men not in actual slavery. Were we whites of the South to remain every way as we are, and our six million blacks to give place to any sort of whites exactly their equals, man for man, in mind, morals, and wealth, provided only that they had tasted two years of American freedom, and were this same system of tyrannies attempted upon them, there would be as bloody an uprising as this continent has ever seen. We can say this quietly. There is not a scruple's weight of present danger. These six million freedmen are dominated by nine million whites immeasurably stronger than they, backed by the virtual consent of thirty-odd millions more. Indeed, nothing but the habit of oppression could make such oppression possible to a people of the intelligence and virtue of our Southern whites, and the invitation to practice it on millions of any other than the children of their former slaves would be spurned with a noble indignation.

Suppose, for a moment, the tables turned. Suppose the courts of our Southern states, while changing no laws requiring the impaneling of jurymen without distinction as to race, etc., should suddenly begin to draw their thousands of jurymen all black, and well-nigh every one of them counting not only himself, but all his race, better than any white man. Assuming that their average of intelligence and morals should be not below that of jurymen as now drawn, would a white man, for all that, choose to be tried in one of those courts? Would he suspect nothing? Could one persuade him that his chances of even justice were all they should be, or all they would be were the court not evading the law in order to sustain an outrageous distinction against him because of the accidents of his birth? Yet only read white man for black man, and black man for white man, and that—I speak as an eyewitness— has been the practice for years, and is still so to-day; an actual emasculation, in the case of six million people both as plaintiff and defendant, of the right of trial by jury.

In this and other practices the outrage falls upon the freedman. Does it stop there? Far from it. It is the first premise of American principles that whatever elevates the lower stratum of the people lifts all the rest, and whatever holds it down holds all down. For twenty years, therefore, the nation has been working to elevate the freedman. It counts this one of the great necessities of the hour. It has poured out its wealth publicly and privately for this purpose. It is confidently expected that it will soon bestow a royal gift of millions for the reduction of the illiteracy so largely shared by the blacks. Our Southern states are, and for twenty years have been, taxing themselves for the same end. The private charities alone of the other states have given twenty millions in the same good cause. Their colored seminaries, colleges, and normal schools dot our whole Southern country, and furnish our public colored schools with a large part of their teachers. All this and much more has been or is being done in order that, for the good of himself and everybody else in the land, the colored man may be elevated as quickly as possible from all the debasements of slavery and semislavery to the full stature and integrity of citizenship. And it is in the face of all this that the adherent of the old régime stands in the way to every public privilege and place—steamer landing, railway platform, theater, concerthall, art display, public library, public school, courthouse, church, everything—flourishing the hot branding-iron of ignominious distinctions. He forbids the freedman to go into the water until *he* is satisfied that he knows how to swim, and for fear he should learn hangs millstones about his neck. This is what we are told is a small matter that will settle itself. Yes, like a roosting curse, until the outraged intelligence of the South lifts its indignant protest against this stupid firing into our own ranks.

I say the outraged intelligence of the South; for there are thousands of Southern-born white men and women in the minority in all these places—in churches, courts, schools, libraries, theaters, concerthalls, and on steamers and railway carriages—who see the wrong and folly of these things, silently blush for them, and withhold their open protests only because their belief is unfortunately stronger in the futility of their counsel than in the power of a just cause. I do not justify their silence; but I affirm their sincerity and their goodly numbers. Of late years, when condemning these evils from the platform in Southern towns, I have repeatedly found that those who I had earlier been told were the men and women in whom the community placed most confidence and pride—they were the ones who, when I had spoken, came forward with warmest hand-grasps and expressions of thanks, and pointedly and cordially justified my every utterance. And were they the young South? Not by half! The graybeards of the old times have always been among them, saying in effect, not by any means as converts, but as fellow discoverers, "Whereas we were blind, now we see."

Another sort among our good Southern people make a similar but feebler admission, but with the time-worn proviso that expediency makes a more imperative demand than law, justice, or logic, and demands the preservation of the old order. Somebody must be outraged, it seems; and if not the freedman, then it must be a highly refined and enlightened race of people constantly offended and grossly discommoded, if not imposed upon, by a horde of tatterdemalions, male and female, crowding into a participation in their reserved privileges. Now, look at this plea. It is simply saying in another way that though the Southern whites far outnumber the blacks, and though we hold every element of power in greater degree than the blacks, and though the larger part of us claim to be sealed by nature as an exclusive upper class, and though we have the courts completely in our own hands, with the police on our right and the prisons on our left, and though we justly claim to be an intrepid people, and though we have a superb military experience, with ninety-nine hundredths of all the military equipment and no scarcity of all the accessories, yet with all the facts behind us we cannot make and enforce that intelligent and approximately just assortment of persons in public places and conveyances on the merits of exterior decency that is made in all other enlightened lands. On such a plea are made a distinction and separation that not only are crude, invidious, humiliating, and tyrannous, but which do not reach their ostensible end or come near it; and all that saves such a plea from being a confession of driveling imbecility is its utter speciousness. It is advanced sincerely; and yet nothing is easier to show than that these distinctions on the line of color are really made not from any necessity, but simply for their own sake—to preserve the old arbitrary supremacy of the master class over the menial without regard to the decency or indecency of appearance or manners in either the white individual or the colored.

See its everyday working. Any colored man gains unquestioned admission into innumerable places the moment he appears as the menial attendant of some white person, where he could not cross the threshold in his own right as a well-dressed and well-behaved master of himself. The contrast is even greater in the case of colored women. There could not be a system which when put into practice would more offensively condemn itself. It does more: it actually creates the confusion it pretends to prevent. It blunts the sensibilities of the ruling class themselves. It waives all strict demand for painstaking in either manners or dress of either master or menial, and, for one result, makes the average Southern railway coach more uncomfortable than the average of railway coaches elsewhere. It prompts the average Southern white passenger to find less offense in the presence of a profane, boisterous, or unclean white person than in that of a quiet, well-behaved colored man or woman attempting to travel on an equal footing with him without a white master or mistress. The holders of the old sentiments hold the opposite choice in scorn. It is only when we go on to say that there are regions where the riotous expulsion of a decent and peaceable colored person is preferred to his inoffensive company, that it may seem necessary to bring in evidence. And yet here again it is *prima facie* evidence; for the following extract was printed in the Selma (Alabama) *Times* not six months ago, and not as a complaint, but as a boast:

A few days since, a negro minister, of this city, boarded the east-bound passenger train on the E. T., V. & G. Railway and took a seat

in the coach occupied by white passengers. Some of the passengers
complained to the conductor and brakemen, and expressed considerable
dissatisfaction that they were forced to ride alongside of a negro. The
railroad officials informed the complainants that they were not au-
thorized to force the colored passenger into the coach set apart for
the negroes, and they would lay themselves liable should they do so.
The white passengers then took the matter in their own hands and
ordered the ebony-hued minister to take a seat in the next coach.
He positively refused to obey orders, whereupon the white men gave
him a sound flogging and forced him to a seat among his own color
and equals. We learned yesterday that the vanquished preacher was
unable to fill his pulpit on account of the severe chastisement inflicted
upon him. Now [says the delighted editor] the query that puzzles is,
"Who did the flogging?"

And as good an answer as we can give is that likely enough they
were some of the men for whom the whole South has come to a
halt to let them get over the "feelings engendered by the war."
Must such men, such acts, such sentiments, stand alone to represent us of the South before an enlightened world? No. I say, as
a citizen of an extreme Southern state, a native of Louisiana, an
ex-Confederate soldier, and a lover of my home, my city, and my
state, as well as of my country, that this is not the best sentiment
in the South, nor the sentiment of her best intelligence; and that
it would not ride up and down that beautiful land dominating and
domineering were it not for its tremendous power as the *traditional*
sentiment of a conservative people. But is not silent endurance
criminal? I cannot but repeat my own words, spoken near the
scene and about the time of this event. Speech may be silvern and
silence golden; but if a lump of gold is only big enough, it can
drag us to the bottom of the sea and hold us there while all the
world sails over us.

The laws passed in the days of compulsory reconstruction requiring "equal accommodations," etc., for colored and white persons were freedmen's follies. On their face they defeated their
ends; for even in theory they at once reduced to half all opportunity for those more reasonable and mutually agreeable self-assort-

ments which public assemblages and groups of passengers find it best to make in all other enlightened countries, making them on the score of conduct, dress, and price. They also led the whites to overlook what they would have seen instantly had these invidious distinctions been made against themselves: that their offense does not vanish at the guarantee against the loss of physical comforts. But we made, and are still making, a mistake beyond even this. For years many of us have carelessly taken for granted that these laws were being carried out in some shape that removed all just ground of complaint. It is common to say, "We allow the man of color to go and come at will, only let him sit apart in a place marked off for him." But marked off how? So as to mark him instantly as a menial. Not by railings and partitions merely, which, raised against any other class in the United States with the same invidious intent, would be kicked down as fast as put up, but by giving him besides, in every instance and without recourse, the most uncomfortable, uncleanest, and unsafest place; and the unsafety, uncleanness, and discomfort of most of these places are a shame to any community pretending to practice public justice. If any one can think the freedman does not feel the indignities thus heaped upon him, let him take up any paper printed for colored men's patronage, or ask any colored man of known courageous utterance. Hear them:

We ask not Congress, nor the Legislature, nor any other power, to remedy these evils, but we ask the people among whom we live. Those who *can* remedy them if they *will*. Those who have a high sense of honor and a deep moral feeling. Those who have one vestige of human sympathy left. . . . Those are the ones we ask to protect us in our weakness and ill-treatments. . . . As soon as the colored man is treated by the white man as a *man,* that harmony and pleasant feeling which should characterize all races which dwell together, shall be the bond of peace between them.

Surely their evidence is good enough to prove their own feelings. We need not lean upon it here for anything else. I shall not bring forward a single statement of fact from them or any of their white friends who, as teachers and missionaries, share many of their humiliations, though my desk is covered with them. But I beg to make the same citation from my own experience that I made last June in the far South. It was this: One hot night in September of last year I was traveling by rail in the state of Alabama. At rather late bed-time there came aboard the train a young mother and her little daughter of three or four years. They were neatly and tastefully dressed in cool, fresh muslins, and as the train went on its way they sat together very still and quiet. At the next station there came aboard a most melancholy and revolting company. In filthy rags, with vile odors and the clanking of shackles and chains, nine penitentiary convicts chained to one chain, and ten more chained to another, dragged laboriously into the compartment of the car where in one corner sat this mother and child, and packed it full, and the train moved on. The keeper of the convicts told me he should take them in that car two hundred miles that night. They were going to the mines. My seat was not in that car, and I stayed in it but a moment. It stank insufferably. I returned to my own place in the coach behind, where there was, and had all the time been, plenty of room. But the mother and child sat on in silence in that foul hole, the conductor having distinctly refused them admission elsewhere because they were of African blood, and not because the mother was, but because she was *not,* engaged at the moment in menial service. Had the child been white, and the mother not its natural but its hired guardian, she could have sat anywhere in the train, and no one would have ventured to object, even had she been as black as the mouth of the coal-pit to which her loathsome fellow passengers were being carried in chains.

Such is the incident as I saw it. But the illustration would be incomplete here were I not allowed to add the comments I made upon it when in June last I recounted it, and to state the two opposite tempers in which my words were received. I said: "These are the facts. And yet you know and I know we belong to communities that, after years of hoping for, are at last taking comfort in the assurance of the nation's highest courts that no law can reach and stop this shameful foul play until we choose to enact a law to that end ourselves. And now the east and north and west of our great and prosperous and happy country, and the rest of the civilized world, as far as it knows our case, are standing and waiting to see what we will write upon the white page of today's and tomorrow's history, now that we are simply on our honor and on the mettle of our far and peculiarly famed Southern instinct. How long, then, shall we stand off from such ringing moral questions as these on the flimsy plea that they have a political value, and, scrutinizing the Constitution, keep saying, 'Is it so nominated in the bond? I cannot find it; 'tis not in the bond.' "

With the temper that promptly resented these words through many newspapers of the neighboring regions there can be no propriety in wrangling. When regions so estranged from the world's thought carry their resentment no further than a little harmless invective, it is but fair to welcome it as a sign of progress. If communities nearer the great centers of thought grow impatient with them, how shall we resent the impatience of these remoter ones when their oldest traditions are, as it seems to them, ruthlessly assailed? There is but one right thing to do: it is to pour in upon them our reiterations of the truth without malice and without stint.

But I have a much better word to say. It is for those who, not voiced by the newspapers around them, showed, both then and constantly afterward in public and private during my two days' subsequent travel and sojourn in the region, by their cordial, frequent, specific approval of my words, that a better intelligence is longing to see the evils of the old régime supplanted by a wiser and more humane public sentiment and practice. And I must repeat my conviction that if the unconscious habit of oppression were not already there, a scheme so gross, irrational, unjust, and inefficient as our present caste distinctions could not find place among a people so generally intelligent and high-minded. I ask attention to their bad influence in a direction not often noticed.

In studying, about a year ago, the practice of letting out public convicts to private lessees to serve out their sentences under private management, I found that it does not belong to all our once slave states nor to all our once seceded states. Only it is no longer in practice outside of them. Under our present condition in the South, it is beyond possibility that the individual black should behave mischievously without offensively rearousing the old sentiments of the still dominant white man. As we have seen, too, the white man virtually monopolizes the jury-box. Add another fact: the Southern states have entered upon a new era of material development. Now, if with these conditions in force the public mind has been captivated by glowing pictures of the remunerative economy of the convict-lease system, and by the seductive spectacle of mines and railways, turnpikes and levees, that everybody wants and nobody wants to pay for, growing apace by convict labor that seems to cost nothing, we may almost assert beforehand that the popular mind will—not so maliciously as unreflectingly—yield to the tremendous temptation to hustle the misbehaving black man into the state prison under extravagant sentence, and sell his labor to the highest bidder who will use him in the construction of public works. For ignorance of the awful condition of these penitentiaries is extreme and general, and the hasty, half-conscious assumption naturally is, that the culprit will survive this term of sentence, and its fierce discipline "teach him to behave himself."

But we need not argue from cause to effect only. Nor need I repeat one of the many painful rumors that poured in upon me the moment I began to investigate this point. The official testimony of the prisons themselves is before the world to establish the conjectures that spring from our reasoning. After the erroneous takings of the census of 1880 in South Carolina had been corrected, the population was shown to consist of about twenty blacks to every thirteen whites. One would therefore look for a preponderance of blacks on the prison lists; and inasmuch as they are a people only twenty years ago released from servile captivity, one would not be surprised to see that preponderance large. Yet, when the actual numbers confront us, our speculations are stopped with a rude shock; for what is to account for the fact that in 1881 there were committed to the state prison at Columbia, South Carolina, 406 colored persons and but 25 whites? The proportion of blacks sentenced to the whole black population was one to every 1488; that of the whites to the white population was but one to every 15,644. In Georgia the white inhabitants decidedly out-number the blacks; yet in the state penitentiary, October 20, 1880, there were 115 whites and 1071 colored; or if we reject the sum-mary of its tables and refer to the tables themselves (for the one does not agree with the other), there were but 102 whites and 1083 colored. Yet of 52 pardons granted in the two years then closing, 22 were to whites and only 30 to blacks. If this be a dark record, what shall we say of the records of lynch law? But for them there is not room here.

A far pleasanter aspect of our subject shows itself when we turn from courts and prisons to the schoolhouse. And the explanation is simple. Were our educational affairs in the hands of that not high average of the community commonly seen in jury boxes, with their transient sense of accountability and their crude notions of public interests, there would most likely be no such pleasant con-trast. But with us of the South, as elsewhere, there is a fairly honest effort to keep the public school interests in the hands of the state's most highly trained intelligence. Hence our public educational work is a compromise between the unprogressive prejudices of the general mass of the whites and the progressive intelligence of their best minds. Practically, through the great majority of our higher educational officers, we are fairly converted to the impera-tive necessity of elevating the colored man intellectually, and are beginning to see very plainly that the whole community is sinned against in every act or attitude of oppression, however gross or however refined.

Yet one thing must be said. I believe it is wise that all have agreed not to handicap education with the race question, but to make a complete surrender of that issue, and let it find adjustment elsewhere first and in the schools last. And yet, in simple truth and justice and in the kindest spirit, we ought to file one exception for that inevitable hour when the whole question must be met. There can be no more real justice in pursuing the freedman's children with humiliating arbitrary distinctions and separations in the school houses than in putting them upon him in other places. If, growing out of their peculiar mental structure, there are good and just reasons for their isolation, by all means let them be proved and known; but it is simply tyrannous to assume them without proof. I know that just here looms up the huge bugbear of social equality. Our eyes are filled with absurd visions of all Shantytown pouring its hordes of unwashed imps into the company and companionship of our own sunny-headed darlings. What utter nonsense! As if our public schools had no gauge of cleanliness, decorum, or moral character! Social equality? What a godsend it would be if the advocates of the old Southern régime could only see that the color line points straight in the direction of social equality by tending toward the equalization of all whites on one side of the line and of all blacks on the other. We may reach the moon some day, not social equality; but the only class that really effects anything toward it are the makers and holders of arbitrary and artificial social distinctions interfering with society's natural self-distribution. Even the little children everywhere are taught, and begin to learn almost with their A B C's, that they will find, and must be guided by, the same variations of the social scale in the public school as out of it; and it is no small mistake to put them or their parents off their guard by this cheap separation on the line of color.

But some will say this is not a purely artificial distinction. We hear much about race instinct. The most of it, I fear, is pure twaddle. It may be there is such a thing. We do not know. It is not proved. And even if it were established, it would not necessarily be a proper moral guide. We subordinate instinct to society's best interests as apprehended in the light of reason. If there is such a thing, it behaves with strange malignity toward the remnants of African blood in individuals principally of our own race, and with singular indulgence to the descendants of—for example—Pocahontas. Of mere race *feeling* we all know there is no scarcity. Who is stranger to it? And as another man's motive of private preference no one has a right to forbid it or require it. But as to its being an instinct, one thing is plain: if there is such an instinct, so far from excusing the malignant indignities practiced in its name, it furnishes their final condemnation; for it stands to reason that just in degree as it is a real thing it will take care of itself.

It has often been seen to do so, whether it is real or imaginary. I have seen in New Orleans a Sunday school of white children every Sunday afternoon take possession of its two rooms immediately upon their being vacated by a black school of equal or somewhat larger numbers. The teachers of the colored school are both white and black, and among the white teachers are young ladies and gentlemen of the highest social standing. The pupils of the two schools are alike neatly attired, orderly, and in every respect inoffensive to each other. I have seen the two races sitting in the same public high school and grammar school rooms, reciting in the same classes and taking recess on the same ground at the same time, without one particle of detriment that any one ever pretended to discover, although the fiercest enemies of the system swarmed about it on every side. And when in the light of these observations I reflect upon the enormous educational task our Southern states have before them, the inadequacy of their own means for performing it, the hoped-for beneficence of the general Government, the sparseness with which so much of our Southern population is distributed over the land, the thousands of school districts where, consequently, the multiplication of schools must involve both increase of expense and reduction of efficiency, I must enter some demurrer to the enforcement of the tyrannous sentiments of the old régime until wise experiments have established better reasons than I have yet heard given.

What need to say more? The question is answered. Is the freedman a free man? No. We have considered his position in a land whence nothing can, and no man has a shadow of right to, drive him, and where he is multiplying as only oppression can multiply a people. We have carefully analyzed his relations to the finer and prouder race, with which he shares the ownership and citizenship of a region large enough for ten times the number of both. Without accepting one word of his testimony, we have shown that the laws made for his protection against the habits of suspicion and oppression in his late master are being constantly set aside, not for their defects, but for such merit as they possess. We have shown that the very natural source of these oppressions is the surviving sentiments of an extinct and now universally execrated institution; sentiments which no intelligent or moral people should harbor a moment after the admission that slavery was a moral mistake. We have shown the outrageousness of these tyrannies in some of their workings, and how distinctly they antagonize every state and national interest involved in the elevation of the colored race. Is it not well to have done so? For, I say again, the question has reached a moment of special importance. The South stands on her honor before the clean equities of the issue. It is no longer whether constitutional amendments, but whether the eternal principles of justice, are violated. And the answer must—it shall—come from the South. And it shall be practical. It will not cost much. We have had a strange experience: the withholding of simple rights has cost us much blood; such concessions of them as we have made have never yet cost a drop. The answer is coming. Is politics in the way? Then let it clear the track or get run over, just as it prefers. But, as I have said over and over to my brethren in the South, I take upon me to say again here, that there is a moral and intellectual intelligence there which is not going to be much longer beguiled out of its moral right of way by questions of political punctilio, but will seek that plane of universal justice and equity which it is every people's duty before God to seek, not along the line of politics—God forbid—but across it and across it and across it as many times as it may lie across the path, until the whole people of every once slaveholding state can stand up as one man, saying, "Is the freedman a free man?" and the whole world shall answer, "Yes."

THOMAS U. DUDLEY

The Right Reverend Thomas Underwood Dudley, Protestant Episcopal bishop of Kentucky, personified the best of the "Silent South," in which George Washington Cable placed his faith. Six months after the appearance of Cable's "The Freedman's Case in Equity" in the *Century Magazine,* Bishop Dudley's essay appeared in the same journal. Dudley referred to Cable's article, quoted from it, and was obviously deeply impressed by it.

Thomas U. Dudley was a native of Richmond, Virginia, and a graduate of the University of Virginia. Following his graduation with an A.M. degree in 1858, he stayed on at the University and taught Latin and Greek until the outbreak of war in 1861. He then volunteered for Confederate army service and was assigned to the commissary department, eventually advancing to the rank of major. At the end of the war he entered the Virginia Theological Seminary in Alexandria, and was ordained in 1868. He served parishes in Harrisonburg, Virginia, and in Baltimore, Maryland, until 1875, when he was elected assistant bishop of the Diocese of Kentucky. Nine years later, he was named bishop, a position he held until his death in 1904. In 1901, he also was named chairman of the House of Bishops, and for years he served as chairman of the committee for evangelistic work among Negroes.

Bishop Dudley was deeply concerned because Negroes increasingly were being placed outside the mainstream of practically every aspect of American life, and he pronounced it to be the duty of every American, North and South, to help uplift them. The argument for deportation he found absurd; while segregation, whether

37

in church or in public transportation, made uplift impossible, because it meant for the Negro "continued and increasing degradation and decay."

There is no record of any outcry against Bishop Dudley for having dared to write as he did. He was, after all, apparently secure in the hierarchy of a church noted for more liberal, though usually paternalistic, views on the Negro. Likewise, Kentucky, from whence he wrote, was scarcely a typical Southern state. Finally, Dudley was far from being the complete racial heretic. He was as fearful of the fruits of miscegenation as the most unsophisticate Southerner, and he held grave doubts that Negroes would ever make any considerable improvement in the domain of morality.

How
Shall We Help
the Negro?

IN discussing this question I do not propose to enter the arena of statistics. I am not quite ready to admit the statement of one writer, that "comparison based on the census of 1870 is utterly worthless as regards the negroes," while yet I do agree that in certain portions of the South it was materially at fault. And although, therefore, the figures of Professor Gilliam, showing that eighty years hence the Southern blacks will nearly double the Southern whites, may not be perfectly accurate, yet, as he further says, "it is morally certain that by that date, and perhaps sooner, the negroes throughout the South will have a great numerical superiority."*

Nor do I propose to enter the lists either as champion or as assailant of the Negro's progress, physical, intellectual, or moral. There can be no question that Mr. [Richard T.] Greener, the first colored graduate of Harvard University, says truly that the Negro is self-supporting, that he adds to the wealth of the country, and that he is accumulating property. As certainly, too, we must admit that the intellectual progress claimed for his race by Mr. Greener is indicated by the existence of "upward of a hundred journals owned and edited by negroes," and by the "number and influence of educated negroes who are now scattered broadcast throughout the South." But on the other hand we note his own declaration that "intemperance, a low standard of morality, an emotional rather than a reflective system of religious ethics, a partial divorce of creed and conduct, and a tendency (by no means confined to

*Reprinted from *Century Magazine*, XXX (June, 1885), 273-80.

negroes) of superficial learning, and of the less desirable elements of character, fitness, or brain, to force their way to the front, are evils which every honest negro must deplore, while sadly admitting their existence."

I recall, as I write, a conversation in New Orleans, in 1880, when I chanced to be placed next to a distinguished federal official at a dinner-table, whereat the wealth and the intelligence of the Crescent City were gathered to do honor to the Chief Justice of the United States. A rather malapropos remark of mine elicited from my companion the confession that he had come to Louisiana as a philanthropist in the days of Reconstruction; that he had been nourished in the faith of human freedom; that his aged father in New Hampshire had prayed with his family morning and evening, since his earliest recollection, that the Negro might be freed. And then he added that the greatest disappointment of his life was to be compelled by experience to acknowledge that the Negro is incapable of development, and that he is utterly incapable of the proper performance of the citizen's duty, either at the polls or in the jury box. Beyond controversy and by the testimony of the educated Negro leaders, and of their partisan friends of the white race, there are still remaining, in spite of all their boasted progress, an ignorance which is simply abysmal, and a moral incapacity before which the lover of humanity, and still more the patriot American, stands appalled. So that I am constrained to fear, and to believe, that Professor Gilliam speaks truth when he adds, as conclusion of the sentence of which I have already quoted a part, that, with numerical superiority, eighty years hence the Negroes throughout the South will have made a "disproportionate gain in wealth and education, and a gain lower still in the domain of morals."

And thirdly, I would say that in seeking for an answer to the dreadful question which keeps repeating itself, "What are you going to do about it?" I shall not for a moment consider the possibility of any emigration of these people which would so much as diminish the cotton crop by a single bale. To my mind it is perfectly absurd to talk of deporting the Negroes of the South to Africa, or to any other country; and it is just as much so to think of setting apart for them a reservation of territory in our own country to which they shall be confined. The fact that by a sacred provision of our Constitution these people are citizens of the United States, and so citizens of each and every state, is sufficient barrier to protect them from forcible migration or emigration; and the further facts that for twenty years they have enjoyed the sweet privileges of American citizenship, that under its protection they have made material progress, that members of their race have sat in the high places as rulers of the nation, and that the school and the ballot-box open a like glorious prospect before the eyes of all—all these things declare that voluntary migration can never take place. No. "The negro has come to America to stay," says Mr. [Samuel C.] Armstrong, in the *North American Review* for July, 1884, and his opinion is corroborated by the opinions of all the educated Negroes given in the symposium whereof he was one.

What then? Here they are, and here they will stay; here we are, and here we mean to stay. Why not? Shall Brobdingnag empty itself of all its giant inhabitants in hurrying dread because Gulliver is come? Or rather, shall Gulliver be alarmed because of the multitude of tiny Lilliputians who crowd the fair land he has found, and madly expatriate himself lest he be destroyed by the pygmies whom he himself has brought there? True, he must recognize, if he be wise, the terrible danger presented by their very number. Doubtless he will feel before long the touch of their restraining hands, if he foolishly lie down to sleep in their midst, and, it may be, will awake to discover that he is conquered. But surely, because of coward fear of such result, he cannot run away and abandon his home. Let us then dismiss both these suggested solutions of our problem as entirely impossible. The Negro cannot be banished from the Southern states, and the white man will not abandon them. The Negro cannot be colonized against his will, nor yet be shut up within any prescribed territory; even did the black man consent thus to dwell apart, when by blood-sealed covenant he is entitled to home and citizenship in each and every state, the enterprising white man would refuse to respect the sanctity of the reservation.

The problem still confronts us. We may not omit to mention still another solution, suggested by no less authority than the great Canon [Alfred E.] Rawlinson, the historian of the monarchies of the ancient world—namely, that the races mingle without restraint, that we make marriages with these people of Canaan, and expect from the union a mixed race mightier and more developed than either factor (such is his promise).

Perhaps it is hardly possible for an American, and least of all an American born to the traditions of the slaveholder, calmly to discuss this proposition to forget the mother who bore him, and to pollute the pure stream of our Caucasian blood by such admixture. But the hope which the English historian has found in the moldy parchments of the far-away East is utterly belied by the results of modern race fusion, which without an exception are adverse to miscegenation. "In no instance," says Professor [Charles A.] Gardiner, "does the mixed people show the mental vigor of the Caucasian parent stock, and in most instances the mental and moral condition of the half-caste is lower even than that of the inferior parent stock." More than this, as is well pointed out by the same writer, Canon Rawlinson, in discussing this question, has fallen into the blunder which in general waits for an Englishman coming to consider anything American. He always thinks of our country as a small island, and would find no fun in Mark Twain's reply to the interviewer "that he was born in New Jersey or Kansas, or just around there." Consequently the great professor thinks of the 6,500,000 Negroes as a mere handful dispersed throughout the 43,000,000 whites, and easily absorbed and assimilated. He is ignorant of, or he ignores, the fact that the Negro must inevitably remain in the Southern states, where even at present the races are about numerically equal, and hence that "a general amalgamation would produce a mulatto stock in which the negro physique and physiognomy would predominate. Whites would be absorbed by negroes, not negroes by whites, and the brain capacity of the mixed race would be little superior to that of the pure negro. Fifty years hence, when negroes will surpass whites as three to one, the mongrel race will represent capacity decidedly inferior to the negro of pure blood." Certainly the white man of the Southern states cannot even consider this remedy for his present ills, this prophylactic against future woes. And let us remember that the Negro looks with just as little good will upon the project to break down the wall of race partition, and make of the twain but one race. Mr. Frederick Douglass seems not to have gained but rather to have lost influence with his people by his recent matrimonial alliance with a white woman; and our own observation fully confirms the statement of Mr. [Joel Chandler] Harris in the *North American Review,* that "whenever the occasion arises the negro is quick to draw the color line, and in some sections of the South, notably in the older cities, there are well-defined social feuds between the blacks and the mulattoes."

What may come in the far-distant future, when by long contact with the superior race the Negro shall have been developed to a higher stage, none can tell. For my own part, believing as I do that "God hath made of one blood all the nations of men," I look for the day when race peculiarities shall be terminated, when the unity of the race shall be manifested. I can find no reason to believe that the great races into which humanity is divided shall remain forever distinct, with their race-marks of color and of form. Centuries hence the red man, the yellow, the white, and the black may all have ceased to exist as such, and in America be found the race combining the bloods of them all; but it must be centuries hence. Instinct and reason, history and philosophy, science and revelation, all alike cry out against the degradation of the race by the free commingling of the tribe which is highest with that which is lowest in the scale of development. The process of selection which nature indicates as the method of most rapid progress indignantly refuses to be thus set at naught. Our temporary ills of today may not be remedied by the permanent wrong of the whole family in heaven and earth.

Still the problem remains, how shall these alien races dwell in safety side by side, each free and unhampered in the enjoyment of life and liberty and in the pursuit of its happiness? They are the descendants of one father, the redeemed children of one God, the citizens of one nation, neighbors with common interests, and yet are separated by the results of centuries of development, physical, mental, and moral—separated by inherited traditions, by the spirit of caste, by the recollection of wrongs done and suffered, though it may be in general as innocent in the perpetrator as in the sufferer. How shall the rights of all be duly guarded? How shall the lower race be lifted up to higher stages of human development, for only so can the rights of the superior race be made secure for the present and for the future, and this is the chiefest right of them who are now cast down?

I answer, by the personal endeavors of individuals of the higher race; by their personal contact with these, their ignorant and untaught neighbors, exhibiting before their wondering eyes in daily life the principles of truth and justice, purity and charity, honesty and courage. Perhaps this may seem to be but the veriest platitude, the gush of sentiment, the twaddle of a maudlin religion, but in all truth and soberness I mean exactly what I say. Let me try to explain more fully.

These people need help, that they may be lifted up. I mean, then, that in my judgment that help must be personal and not official, the hand of a friend rather than the club of an officer, the patient counsel of a neighbor rather than the decree of a court, the enactment of a Congress, or the proclamation of a President. The solemn sanctions of the organic law are thrown round about this liberty, and the robe of citizenship, full, perfect, and complete, with never seam nor rent, has been put upon it. The courts have declared its inviolable character, and this decree affirms the Negro, the liberated slave, a citizen. But does the declaration make him such? I mean does it, can it impart the intelligent life, the moral consciousness which shall vivify the dead mass and make it a helpful member of the body politic? We have had declarations from every department of the government that the Negro is a citizen; but they are as powerless to effect their purpose as were the oft-repeated acts of the Confederate Congress to make the paper dollar worth more than two cents; as nugatory and vain as the old-time legislation of Virginia that there should be a town at such and such a designated cross road. The Negro is a citizen, and he has the rights under the Constitution and the laws that any white man has; and yet he needs help, though it may be the black and white demagogues would dislike him to think so—he needs help, personal, individual, patient, loving help, that he may be fitted to exercise his covenanted rights, and to do the duties which these rights impose.

Let us turn for a moment to another sphere of life wherein he now plays an independent part. I mean the Christian church, using the term in its widest popular signification, as including all organized bodies of Christian disciples. When the war was ended, nowhere was the newly acquired freedom more quickly active than in the organization of religious societies among the Negroes. The white pastors who for so many years had ministered unto them were cast out without ceremony; the guidance of the experienced and trusty Christian white men was repudiated, and in each congregation the government was given exclusively to black men; and while we may hesitate to believe that "the Lord gave the word," yet certainly, as the psalmist says, great was the company of the preachers, "those that published." In very many places, because of the rapid influx of the liberated slaves into the towns, new and large meetinghouses were erected and new congregations organized. Utterly ignorant men, gifted with a fatal fluency of speech, unable often to read the Bible in English, much less in its original tongues, became the blind guides of blind followers; and the result is that in some places within my personal knowledge a revival meeting has been going on every night since the surrender of Johnston's army. The orgies of their so-called worship are such as to cause any Christian man to blush for the caricature of our holy religion therein portrayed. As the years passed by, the congregations were associated under the particular polity to which they happened to belong, preacher and people being in general alike ignorant of the features and the claims of all. Conferences meet, general associations are held, bishops, presiding elders, professors, and doctors in divinity assemble, and there is much oratory; and alas, it is too often made plain that the teachers are themselves ignorant of the very first principles of the gospel of Christ. Not that I mean to say that these men cannot all talk glibly in slang theological phrase about the eternal verities—for they can. And still less would I be understood as saying that there are not among these, my colored brothers, men whom I rejoice to call brothers, and from whom I rejoice to learn, not the science of the books, but the glorious guarantee of my Christian hope in their vital apprehension of the Father's love. And others there are now fully equal in learning to the average white minister, but these are few and far separated. But I believe that in general it were as wise to take the infant-class of a well-taught Sunday school, with one of the older boys as its preacher, and set it up as an independent church, as so to constitute a body of the average Negroes in the Southern states.

I hold that those Christian bodies have acted most unwisely who have set off the Negroes belonging to their communions as independent churches, and so have taken from them the enlightening instruction, the helpful guidance, the pastoral care of the white men. I know that it was hard to resist the importunity of the Negroes, eager thus to display their capacity as leaders, organizers, and preachers, backed as they were by the thoughtless mob behind them. I know, too, that it was taking a burden from shoulders already heavily laden, thus to shift the responsibility of giving religious instruction to this great multitude. But I know equally well that the result has been evil, that the religious development of the Negro race in our Southern states has been hindered by the separation. Just a year and a half ago there was held in the city of Louisville, Kentucky, a meeting of colored ministers, and the report of their proceedings, published in a newspaper conducted by Negroes, affords a most melancholy evidence of the fact that, separated from their white brethren, these, the leaders, had degenerated, and had ceased to realize, if they had ever fully done so, that the end and object of religion is morality, the uplifting of men into the likeness of God: for this report portrays ministers of the gospel charging one another with the grossest violations of the moral law! "If the light that is in thee be darkness, how great is that darkness!" If the teachers of religion, the exponents of the moral law, be thus liable to mutual recrimination, what must be the condition of the great mass of their followers! Declared Christians as declared citizens, they need help—personal, individual, tender, persistent—to enable them to become such in any true sense. The mistake of the United States government has been repeated by some of the Christian denominations. Perhaps it was inevitable, but at all events it has taken away one of the chief agencies which the white man could employ to educate the black man to a true conception of citizenship; and alas, as the years go by, it must be more and more difficult for us to gain control of it again. Is it not worthy of consideration by the Southern men who are the ministers and leaders of the denominations with which these people are most largely associated, at least in name, whether they cannot make the bond a closer one, and so be enabled, at least indirectly, to shape the policy of their weaker brethren? Responsibility must be heavy in proportion to opportunity, and that responsibility cannot be put away by a mere yielding to the clamor of an ignorant populace, demanding that it may rest upon them and their children.

To return to the more general discussion of our question, I ask, by whom should this personal interest in the Negro be felt and shown? And the answer is, of course, patent, that the duty rests upon all Americans alike. We need not reopen the old sore of the original importation of Africans into our country, and allege, as we might, that the guilt of it, if there be guilt, rests upon the ancestors of our New England cousins, rather than upon the fathers of us Southern people. Further, it goes without saying that the federal government which added this great number to our roll of citizens should, in common fairness, do all that it may do to help them to the attainment of civic capacity, and to help us so to help them. And if it be questioned whether the constitutional power to do this thing exist, it would seem to be sufficient answer in equity that it must be a part of the power by which emancipation was effected. But in a word, because the citizen of one state is a citizen of every other, and because, if one member of our body politic suffer, all the others by the very law of our being must suffer also, it follows that from every American white man this help may be rightfully expected. But to the men of the South, my own dear kinsmen after the flesh, I would speak, and say that of necessity the burden of this labor must fall upon us. Hard it may seem to some of us that, despoiled of our property for which our money was paid, and whose protection was guaranteed to our fathers, placed under the very feet of our former slaves by the conquering power of the federal government and the chicanery and fraud of unscrupulous white men, we should now be called upon to give our personal care, our time, our sympathy, and our meager resources to the development of these semi-barbarians up to true manhood and intelligent citizenship. But be it hard, 'tis true. The burden rests upon us, and we cannot put it away. The love of our whole country demands it; that special regard we cannot but feel for the well-being and advancement of our own people and our own sunny home demands it; recognition of the truth of human brother-hood—that revelation of Jesus Christ and that last result of sociological study—demands it.

And how and where shall we begin? I answer, "every man in the deep of his own heart," by building there, firm and stable, the conviction that the Negro is a man and a citizen; that the conditions of our life are all changed; that old things are passed away, and that the new things which are come to us demand, with an authority which may not be gainsaid, the effort of mind and heart and hand for the uplifting of the Negro, lest, if he be left lying in his degradation, he pull us down to his defilement. Nay, we must build higher than this, even the conviction that it is the will of God that the nobler shall be evolved from the ignoble, that the race shall progress toward his likeness; and from the summit of this lofty conception we can look out and see the work to be done, and there we can breathe the pure air of heaven, and get inspiration for its performance, though it cost self-denial and self-sacrifice. Here we must begin in ridding our hearts of the feeling of caste, which has made them its citadel for generations.

But let it be clearly understood that I have not the least reference to the social status of the freedman when I so speak. That mysterious thing which we call "society" will ever take care of itself, and my taking away the pariah badge which caste has affixed to the Negro is by no means the presentation to him of a card of invitation to the soirée in my parlor. No man has an inherent right to be admitted into a circle which is in general defined by equality of distance from some fixed point of refinement, culture, leisure, or wealth. Undoubtedly it seems to be too true that the door of admission in our American life is generally to be unlocked by the golden key, whatever be the hand that holds it. And yet, after all, this seeming welcome to the almighty dollar is in reality accorded to the qualifications which wealth can supply, even culture, leisure, and refinement, and the community of interests with those possessing like advantages. But certainly no man or woman has any indefeasible right to social recognition, and its refusal is not a denial of equity. The time may come, and will, when the prejudices now apparently invincible shall have been conquered by the changed characteristics of the race now under the social ban. Society, then as now organized upon the basis of community of interests, congeniality of tastes, and equality of position, will exclude the multitude who cannot speak its shibboleth; but there will be no color line of separation. If the aspirate be duly sounded, the thickness of the lips that frame the word shall be no hindrance to the social welcome. When shall this be? Ah, when? In the far-distant future it may be; and equally it may be that our great-grandchildren shall behold such a social revolution as will open wide the drawingrooms of Washington to the black men who have been honored guests in the palaces of England and of France. But whether it shall ever be or not is no point in the discussion I am making; for immediate social recognition is not an equitable demand, nor yet a necessary factor in the development of the Negro race, which is his right and our only safety.

But poverty and ignorance are no barrier in the way of the elevation of any white man in America, nor yet the obscurity or even degradation of his origin. Though in infancy he may have lain "among the pots," yes, and the pigs of an Irish hovel, yet in this favored land of equal rights no arbitrary distinction shall stand in the way of his education into a cultivated refinement that shall be as "the wings of a dove covered with silver," nor prevent that his trained powers shall cover "her feathers with yellow gold." Why shall a different condition hedge about the black man because, forsooth, the hovel he was born in was in Carolina rather than Galway, and the pigs, his playmates, had a private pen?

But further, the helping hand of intelligent wealth never fails to be outstretched to smooth the path of the indigent white boy whose honesty and capacity and diligence give promise of a successful career. Our annals are full of splendid instances of the success attending such personal effort to further the progress of the struggling child of poverty, and even of shame. Why shall not these annals record in the future the names of black boys thus developed, by the personal care of members of the higher race, into a manhood as noble and as beneficent? Is it that there is lacking the capacity for development? Such opinion will hardly be expressed by any intelligent observer in our day. The scholars and orators, the mechanics and accountants, of pure Negro blood, moral and upright, trusty and trusted, who have been made here in America, flatly contradict any such assumption. True, they are few in number; true, that in general the members of this race have as yet acquired but the little learning which is so dangerous; true, that left to themselves, under leaders of their own race, they have in almost every case made grievous failure, have made loud boasting of an uplifting which was just high enough to display their grotesque ugliness. Surely these results were to be expected in the circumstances attending their effort for self-advancement. Yet, one man of high character and real education is enough to prove capacity. America can furnish many such, and of the great number which England offers, I cite one that is a crucial, splendid instance, and which alone must satisfy. An English cruiser overhauls a slave ship homeward bound with its cargo of living treasure. The hatches are burst open, and the bondmen come forth from the nameless horrors of the middle passage just begun. Among them is a boy of typical African feature and form, who, for some cause, attracts the notice of a man who loves his fellow men; and when the liberated are carried back to roam again as free savages their native wilds, he is taken to England, that culture may develop the god-like nature in which he was created, that by contact with individuals of the higher kingdom this denizen of the lower may be lifted up. Today that boy is the Bishop of the Niger, governing and guiding the missionary work of the Church of England in all the vast region of West Africa.

Capacity is not lacking, but help is needed, the help, I repeat, which the intelligence of the superior race must give by careful selection and personal contact with the selected. Does not our mother nature teach us that this is the only process offering prospect of success, such being her method of procedure in her constant working under the Creator's law? "The plant," says Mr. Drummond, "stretches down to the dead world beneath it, touches its minerals and gases with its mystery of life, and brings them up ennobled and transformed to the living sphere." "The kingdom of heaven," said Jesus of Nazareth, "is like leaven which a woman took and hid in three measures of meal till the whole was leavened." The teaching of nature and of the Lord of nature alike declare that the leavened mass, the alive, must touch that which is dead to impart of its life; the higher must stoop to touch the lower, and its contact must be long continued, individual, personal, real, if the lower is to be carried up to the superior sphere. And the Christian philosopher, the greatest expounder of the religion of Jesus Christ, sums it all up into one command, when he charges those who would help forward the coming of the kingdom of the Christ, wherein shall be universal brotherhood among Christian men: "Be not high-minded, but condescend to men of low estate."

The separation of the Negro race from the white means for the Negro continued and increasing degradation and decay. His hope, his salvation, must come from association with that people among whom he dwells, but from whose natural guidance and care he has been separated largely by the machinations of unscrupulous demagogues. These care not a straw for his elevation, but would mount on his shoulders to place and power. They find their opportunity in the natural, indeed inevitable, estrangement of the liberated slave from his former master; and they are more than content to keep the Negro in thriftless ignorance, that he may continue their subservient follower. Certainly it was natural that these new-created citizens should join themselves to the leaders whose hands had broken the shackles of their slavery. Instinct prompted such alliance, and the fawning words of the cringing flatterer found ready acceptance and belief, when he told of the old master's desire again to fasten the chain which he, the orator, had broken with the tools in his carpet-bag. 'Twas pitiable to see the sorrow of many of these people when the announcement was made that a Democrat had been elected President, for they had been taught to believe that such an event meant their restoration to the condition of servitude. And it was cruel to witness, as I did, the sportive mockery of unthinking white men, who tortured the Negroes by the assertion of ownership, and in some cases went through the mockery of selling them at auction. But is not now the opportunity of Southern white men to reëstablish the bond of friendship with their former slaves, and to prove to them that our interests are identical? The issue of the last presidential election has opened even the blindest eyes to see that the freedom of their race is in no sense dependent upon the continued supremacy of the Republican party, but is assured by the organic law which no political party can change. The time is come that we may make them know that our desire is to help them along the road to prosperity and happiness, even as we ask them to help us. The time is come for honest, manly effort to teach them that in our union is the only hope of both races; that separated from us, their neighbors and friends, they must retrograde toward the barbarism whence they are sprung, and, that then, alas, we might be compelled to wage relentless war against them for our own preservation. The white men of the South must help the Negro politically, if they would be helped by him, and first of all must give him assurance of honest purpose, by the removal of the ban which prejudice has established, and treat as a freeman him whom the Constitution and the laws declare free.

I am sure that particular cases of his present hardship will readily occur to all; notably one to which Mr. Cable called such vigorous attention in *The Century* for January of the current year. I could but think of it with a blush as I journeyed a little while ago on a south-bound railway train, and saw a tidy, modest, and intelligent black woman restricted to a car which, when she entered it, was about as full of oaths and obscenity as of the foul vapor compounded of the fumes of tobacco and of whisky. At the same station came aboard the train two white women, evidently less intelligent, less refined in manner, and by no means so cleanly dressed; and they were admitted to the privileges of the so-called ladies' car, which, under the usual interpretation, means merely "white people's car." Is this just? Is this equitable? Must not any possible elevation of the Negro race by our efforts have a beginning in the removal of such flagrant wrongs as this?

Again, I notice, as perhaps falling more constantly under my own observation, the cruel prejudice which stands like an angry sentinel at our church doors to warn away these people whom we yet declare to be children of the one Father. Certainly it is no injustice to anybody that a number of Christians shall join together for the erection of a church and the provision of services; and in the architecture they shall select, the form of worship they shall employ, the doctrines they shall have proclaimed, they may please their own fancy or conscience, and no man has a right to complain. More than this, there is no more wrong in the appropriation of particular seats to particular persons who choose to pay therefor a price greater or less. Still further, the American Christian's pew is his castle, if he please to make it such, and no stranger may with impunity invade it. The religious club may, like other associations of that species, grant admission to the privileges of its club house only by card, and nobody has a right to complain. But when the religious club sets up a claim to be the visible kingdom of God on earth, whose mission and ground of being are the making known the glad tidings to the poor and the outcast, what absurdity of contradiction in such exclusive selfishness! The congregations of Christian people in our country seem with one accord to recognize their duty as their highest pleasure, and welcome most gladly all who come to join their prayers and praises and to hear their teacher. Ushers will confront you with smiling welcome at the door of any church in the land, and conduct you to a seat, though you be introduced by no member. Your manhood is your right to enter—*if only your face is white.* Is this just? Is this equitable? Above all, is this Christian? It is but a foolish dread which justifies such distinction on the ground that, once admitted, the Negro would take possession and rule the church. Social sympathies, we know very well, have perhaps most to do with the gathering of any congregation of regular worshipers; sympathies which, as we have seen, arise from equality of material condition, community of tastes, participation in the same daily life. Why do we not fear to welcome as occasional visitor the white man or woman of low degree? Why does not like danger in their case restrain our Christian hospitality? Is the Negro more pushing and self-assertive than the rude white man? Nay, rather is he not by his very pride of race, and his natural resentment of the white man's contumely, unwilling even to join with him in doing homage to the one King? This is but a pretext to excuse the conduct which, in our heart of hearts, we know to proceed from the old root of bitterness—the feeling of caste which demands that the liberated slave shall be forever a menial.

I charge the Christian white men of the South to mark that the effect of this separation, on which we have insisted, has helped to drive these people into a corresponding exclusiveness, and is constantly diminishing the influence of our Christian thinkers upon their belief and their practice. And twenty years of the separate life of these churches of the black man have made plain the inevitable tendency. They have colleges and newspapers, missionary societies and mammoth meeting houses; they have baptized multitudes, and they maintain an unbroken revival; and yet confessedly the end of the commandment, the morality, the godlikeness which all religion is given to attain, is farther away than at the beginning. Their religion is a superstition, their sacraments are fetiches, their worship is a wild frenzy, and their morality a shame. I have myself heard the stewards of a city congregation reviling a country visitor because she always selected the Communion Sunday as the occasion of her visit, "that she might drink their good wine"; and the soft impeachment was not denied.

True, there are white people equally ignorant of the first principles of Christianity, and whose moral character is equally destitute of religious influence; but would it be wise or safe or Christian to let them organize separate communions, to give them up to their blind guides? This is all I plead for, that separation from us is for the Negro destruction, and perhaps for us as well. Therefore we must help them, teach them, guide them, lift them up; and that we may do so, we must treat them as men.

Difficulties frown upon us as we enter this path. Our friends will look at us with eyes askant, and it may be will speak bitter words whose sting will wound; but this we can bear, for their conduct will not much damage our work, and we can believe that by and by they will see the truth and love it. But harder to overcome, and of direful influence upon the very beginning of their labor who labor for peace, are the black demagogues who have learned from their white partners that the ignorance of their brethren must be the mother of devotion to their selfish interests; that their unreasoning hostility to their white neighbors is the cement which fastens securely their dependence upon them.

Preachers and politicians, each being as much the one as the other, will resent and resist our effort to open the blind eyes that they may see their glorious freedom in the Church and in the state. Pride of race will be summoned to resist the alien; grateful recollection will turn away to the white men who came a score of years ago kindly to become their governors and congressmen and senators. The ignorant ranter who has held thousands spellbound while he pictured the torment of the flaming lake, and called his hearers away to the sensuous delights of a Mohammedan paradise, will not freely consent to the introduction of preachers having intelligence, learning, and rational piety. But the truth will prevail at the last, if only it can find an entrance. We must carry it to them ourselves, despite all opposition. We must put away from us the devil's delusion that by declaring them citizens we have made them really such; that in giving them the alphabet of the Christian faith we have fitted them to dwell apart and alone.

I noticed in the brave and manly plea of Mr. Cable, already mentioned, these words, quoted from a newspaper published by black men:

We ask not Congress, nor the Legislature, nor any other power, to remedy these evils, but we ask the people among whom we live. Those who *can* remedy them if they *will*. Those who have a high sense of honor and a deep moral feeling. Those who have one vestige of human sympathy left. . . . Those are the ones we ask to protect us in our weakness and ill-treatments. . . . As soon as the colored man is treated by the white man *as a man,* that harmony and pleasant feeling which should characterize all races which dwell together, shall be the bond of peace between them.

White men of the South, what answer shall we, the intelligent, the cultured, the powerful, the inheritors of noble traditions and of splendid ideas—what answer, I ask in the name of God, of freedom and of humanity, shall we make to these men?

THOMAS E. WATSON

Tom Watson was a "scrawny, red-headed, agrarian avenger" determined to create a new political party which would unite poor white and Negro farmers in the bonds of common self-interest. Both were in the ditch together, yet kept apart, said Watson, "that you may be separately fleeced of your earnings. You are made to hate each other because upon that hatred is rested the keystone of the arch of financial despotism which enslaves you both. You are deceived and blinded that you may not see how this race antagonism perpetuates a monetary system which beggars you both."

When his essay was published in the *Arena* in 1892, Tom Watson was a Congressman from Georgia, elected upon a Farmers Alliance platform within the Democratic party which he deserted to join the new People's or Populist party. Two months later Watson was defeated in a bid for reelection as a result of the Democratic legislature's having gerrymandered his district, leading to an election which has been accurately characterized as a "solemn farce."

While it is perhaps true that Watson called for class warfare, he still enjoys the unique distinction of being the only Southern politician who sought to unite the oppressed of both races in a program of self-interest, without regard to skin color and past political affiliation. In the question of social equality, he had no interest, for that was "a thing each citizen decides for himself." For some years after 1892 Watson remained a champion of equal political rights, at least, for the Negro, but by 1904 he was advocating disfranchisement of black men! Frustrated, embittered, and disappointed, the "wild man from Hickory Hill" had been conquered by his Negro "Nemesis." The Tom Watson who might have been a great man was dead; Watson the hater of Negroes, Jews, and Catholics lived and fought on for another eighteen years.

The
Negro Question
in the South

THE Negro Question in the South has been for nearly thirty years a source of danger, discord, and bloodshed. It is an ever-present irritant and menace.*

Several millions of slaves were told that they were the prime cause of the civil war; that their emancipation was the result of the triumph of the North over the South; that the ballot was placed in their hands as a weapon of defence against their former masters; that the war-won political equality of the black man with the white, must be asserted promptly and aggressively, under the leadership of adventurers who had swooped down upon the conquered section in the wake of the Union armies.

No one, who wishes to be fair, can fail to see that, in such a condition of things, strife between the freedman and his former owner was inevitable. In the clashing of interests and of feelings, bitterness was born. The black man was kept in a continual fever of suspicion that we meant to put him back into slavery. In the assertion of his recently acquired privileges, he was led to believe that the best proof of his being on the right side of any issue was that his old master was on the other. When this was the case, he felt easy in his mind. But if, by any chance, he found that he was voting the same ticket with his former owner, he at once became reflective and suspicious. In the irritable temper of the times, a whispered warning from a Northern "carpetbagger," having no justification in rhyme or reason, outweighed with him a carload of sound argument and earnest expostulation from the

*Reprinted from the *Arena*, VI (September, 1892), 540–50.

man whom he had known all his life; who had hunted with him through every swamp and wooded upland for miles around; who had wrestled and run foot-races with him in the "Negro quarters" on many a Saturday afternoon; who had fished with him at every "hole" in the creek; and who had played a thousand games of "marble" with him under the cool shade of the giant oaks which, in those days, sheltered a home they had both loved.

In brief, the end of the war brought changed relations and changed feelings. Heated antagonisms produced mutual distrust and dislike—ready, at any accident of unusual provocation on either side, to break out into passionate and bloody conflict.

Quick to take advantage of this deplorable situation, the politicians have based the fortunes of the old parties upon it. Northern leaders have felt that at the cry of "Southern outrage" they could not only "fire the northern heart," but also win a unanimous vote from the colored people. Southern politicians have felt that at the cry of "Negro domination" they could drive into solid phalanx every white man in all the Southern states.

Both the old parties have done this thing until they have constructed as perfect a slot machine as the world ever saw. Drop the old, worn nickel of the "party slogan" into the slot, and the machine does the rest. You might beseech a Southern white tenant to listen to you upon questions of finance, taxation, and transportation; you might demonstrate with mathematical precision that herein lay his way out of poverty into comfort; you might have him "almost persuaded" to the truth, but if the merchant who furnished his farm supplies (at tremendous usury) or the town politician (who never spoke to him excepting at election times) came along and cried "Negro rule!" the entire fabric of reason and common sense which you had patiently constructed would fall, and the poor tenant would joyously hug the chains of an actual wretchedness rather than do any experimenting on a question of mere sentiment.

Thus the Northern Democrats have ruled the South with a rod of iron for twenty years. We have had to acquiesce when the time-

honored principles we loved were sent to the rear and new doctrines and policies we despised were engrafted on our platform. All
this we have had to do to obtain the assistance of Northern
Democrats to prevent what was called "Negro supremacy." In
other words, the Negro has been as valuable a portion of the stock
in trade of a Democrat as he was of a Republican. Let the South
ask relief from Wall Street; let it plead for equal and just laws
on finance; let it beg for mercy against crushing taxation, and
Northern Democracy, with all the coldness, cruelty, and subtlety
of Mephistopheles, would hint "Negro rule!" and the white farmer
and laborer of the South had to choke down his grievance and
march under Tammany's orders.

Reverse the statement, and we have the method by which the
black man was managed by the Republicans.

Reminded constantly that the North had emancipated him; that
the North had given him the ballot; that the North had upheld
him in his citizenship; that the South was his enemy, and meant
to deprive him of his suffrage and put him "back into slavery,"
it is no wonder he has played as nicely into the hands of the
Republicans as his former owner has played into the hands of the
Northern Democrats.

Now consider: here were two distinct races dwelling together,
with political equality established between them by law. They
lived in the same section; won their livelihood by the same pursuits; cultivated adjoining fields on the same terms; enjoyed together the bounties of a generous climate; suffered together the
rigors of cruelly unjust laws; spoke the same language; bought and
sold in the same market; classified themselves into churches under
the same denominational teachings; neither race antagonizing the
other in any branch of industry; each absolutely dependent on the
other in all the avenues of labor and employment; and yet, instead
of being allies, as every dictate of reason and prudence and self-
interest and justice said they should be, they were kept apart, in
dangerous hostility, that the sordid aims of partisan politics
might be served!

So completely has this scheme succeeded that the Southern black man almost instinctively supports any measure the Southern white man condemns, while the latter almost universally antagonizes any proposition suggested by a Northern Republican. We have, then, a solid South as opposed to a solid North; and in the South itself, a solid black vote against the solid white.

That such a condition is most ominous to both sections and both races, is apparent to all.

If we were dealing with a few tribes of red men or a few sporadic Chinese, the question would be easily disposed of. The Anglo-Saxon would probably do just as he pleased, whether right or wrong, and the weaker man would go under.

But the Negroes number 8,000,000. They are interwoven with our business, political, and labor systems. They assimilate with our customs, our religion, our civilization. They meet us at every turn—in the fields, the shops, the mines. They are a part of our system, and they are here to stay.

Those writers who tediously wade through census reports to prove that the Negro is disappearing, are the most absurd mortals extant. The Negro is not disappearing. A Southern man who looks about him and who sees how rapidly the colored people increase, how cheaply they can live, and how readily they learn, has no patience whatever with those statistical lunatics who figure out the final disappearance of the Negro one hundred years hence. The truth is, that the "black belts" in the South are getting blacker. The race is mixing less than it ever did. Mulattoes are less common (in proportion) than during the times of slavery. Miscegenation is further off (thank God) than ever. Neither the blacks nor the whites have any relish for it. Both have a pride of race which is commendable, and which, properly directed, will lead to the best results for both. The home of the colored man is chiefly with us in the South, and there he will remain. It is there he is founding churches, opening schools, maintaining newspapers, entering the professions, serving on juries, deciding doubtful elections, drilling as a volunteer soldier, and piling up a cotton crop which amazes the world.

This preliminary statement is made at length that the gravity of the situation may be seen. Such a problem never confronted any people before.

Never before did two distinct races dwell together under such conditions.

And the problem is, can these two races, distinct in color, distinct in social life, and distinct as political powers, dwell together in peace and prosperity?

Upon a question so difficult and delicate no man should dogmatize—nor dodge. The issue is here; grows more urgent every day, and must be met.

It is safe to say that the present status of hostility between the races can only be sustained at the most imminent risk to both. It is leading by logical necessity to results which the imagination shrinks from contemplating. And the horrors of such a future can only be averted by honest attempts at a solution of the question which will be just to both races and beneficial to both.

Having given this subject much anxious thought, my opinion is that the future happiness of the two races will never be assured until the political motives which drive them asunder, into two distinct and hostile factions, can be removed. There must be a new policy inaugurated, whose purpose is to allay the passions and prejudices of race conflict, and which makes its appeal to the sober sense and honest judgment of the citizen regardless of his color.

To the success of this policy two things are indispensable—a common necessity acting upon both races, and a common benefit assured to both—without injury or humiliation to either.

Then, again, outsiders must let us alone. We must work out our own salvation. In no other way can it be done. Suggestions of federal interference with our elections postpone the settlement and render our task the more difficult. Like all free people, we love home rule, and resent foreign compulsion of any sort. The Northern leader who really desires to see a better state of things in the South, puts his finger on the hands of the clock and forces them backward every time he intermeddles with the question. This is the literal truth; and the sooner it is well understood, the sooner we can accomplish our purpose.

What is that purpose? To outline a policy which compels the support of a great body of both races, from those motives which imperiously control human action, and which will thus obliterate forever the sharp and unreasoning political divisions of to-day.

The white people of the South will never support the Republican party. This much is certain. The black people of the South will never support the Democratic party. This is equally certain.

Hence, at the very beginning, we are met by the necessity of new political alliances. As long as the whites remain solidly Democratic, the blacks will remain solidly Republican.

As long as there was no choice, except as between the Democrats and the Republicans, the situation of the two races was bound to be one of antagonism. The Republican party represented everything which was hateful to the whites; the Democratic party, everything which was hateful to the blacks.

Therefore a new party was absolutely necessary. It has come, and it is doing its work with marvellous rapidity.

Why does a Southern Democrat leave his party and come to ours?

Because his industrial condition is pitiably bad; because he struggles against a system of laws which have almost filled him with despair; because he is told that he is without clothing because he produces too much cotton, and without food because corn is too plentiful; because he sees everybody growing rich off the products of labor except the laborer; because the millionnaires who manage the Democratic party have contemptuously ignored his plea for a redress of grievances and have nothing to say to him beyond the cheerful advice to "work harder and live closer."

Why has this man joined the People's party? Because the same grievances have been presented to the Republicans by the farmer of the West, and the millionnaires who control that party have replied to the petition with the soothing counsel that the Republican farmer of the West should "work more and talk less."

Therefore, if he were confined to a choice between the two old parties, the question would merely be (on these issues) whether the pot were larger than the kettle—the color of both being precisely the same.

The key to the new political movement called the People's party has been that the Democratic farmer was as ready to leave the Democratic ranks as the Republican farmer was to leave the Republican ranks. In exact proportion as the West received the assurance that the South was ready for a new party, it has moved. In exact proportion to the proof we could bring that the West had broken Republican ties, the South has moved. *Without* a decided break in both sections, neither would move. *With* that decided break, both moved.

The very same principle governs the race question in the South. The two races can never act together permanently, harmoniously, beneficially, till each race demonstrates to the other a readiness to leave old party affiliations and to form new ones, based upon the profound conviction that, in acting together, both races are seeking new laws which will benefit both. On no other basis under heaven can the Negro Question be solved.

Now, suppose that the colored man were educated upon these questions just as the whites have been; suppose he were shown that his poverty and distress came from the same sources as ours; suppose we should convince him that our platform principles assure him an escape from the ills he now suffers, and guarantee him the fair measure of prosperity his labor entitles him to receive,— would he not act just as the white Democrat who joined us did? Would he not abandon a party which ignores him as a farmer and laborer; which offers him no benefits of an equal and just financial system; which promises him no relief from oppressive taxation; which assures him of no legislation which will enable him to obtain a fair price for his produce?

Granting to him the same selfishness common to us all; granting him the intelligence to know what is best for him and the desire to attain it, why would he not act from that motive just as the white farmer has done?

That he would do so, is as certain as any future event can be made. Gratitude may fail; so may sympathy and friendship and generosity and patriotism; but in the long run, self-interest *always* controls. Let it once appear plainly that it is to the interest of a colored man to vote with the white man, and he will do it. Let it plainly appear that it is to the interest of the white man that the vote of the Negro should supplement his own, and the question of having that ballot freely cast and fairly counted, becomes vital to the *white man*. He will see that it is done.

Now let us illustrate: Suppose two tenants on my farm; one of them white, the other black. They cultivate their crops under precisely the same conditions. Their labors, discouragements, burdens, grievances, are the same.

The white tenant is driven by cruel necessity to examine into the causes of his continued destitution. He reaches certain conclusions which are not complimentary to either of the old parties. He leaves the Democracy in angry disgust. He joins the People's party. Why? Simply because its platform recognizes that he is badly treated and proposes to fight his battle. Necessity drives him from the old party, and hope leads him into the new. In plain English, he joins the organization whose declaration of principles is in accord with his conception of what he needs and justly deserves.

Now go back to the colored tenant. His surroundings being the same and his interests the same, why is it impossible for him to reach the same conclusions? Why is it unnatural for him to go into the new party at the same time and with the same motives?

Cannot these two men act together in peace when the ballot of the one is a vital benefit to the other? Will not political friendship be born of the necessity and the hope which is common to both? Will not race bitterness disappear before this common suffering and this mutual desire to escape it? Will not each of these citizens feel more kindly for the other when the vote of each defends the home of both? If the white man becomes convinced that the Democratic party has played upon his prejudices, and has used his quiescence to the benefit of interests adverse to his own, will he not despise the leaders who seek to perpetuate the system?

The People's party will settle the race question. First, by enacting the Australian ballot system. Second, by offering to white and black a rallying point which is free from the odium of former discords and strifes. Third, by presenting a platform immensely beneficial to both races and injurious to neither. Fourth, by making it to the *interest* of both races to act together for the success of the platform. Fifth, by making it to the *interest* of the colored man to have the same patriotic zeal for the welfare of the South that the whites possess.

Now to illustrate. Take two planks of the People's party platform: that pledging a free ballot under the Australian system and that which demands a distribution of currency to the people upon pledges of land, cotton, etc.

The guaranty as to the vote will suit the black man better than the Republican platform, because the latter contemplates federal interference, which will lead to collisions and bloodshed. The Democratic platform contains no comfort to the Negro, because, while it denounces the Republican programme, as usual, it promises nothing which can be specified. It is a generality which does not even possess the virtue of being "glittering."

The People's party, however, not only condemns federal interference with elections, but also distinctly commits itself to the method by which every citizen shall have his constitutional right to the free exercise of his electoral choice. We pledge ourselves to isolate the voter from all coercive influences and give him the free and fair exercise of his franchise under state laws.

Now couple this with the financial plank which promises equality in the distribution of the national currency, at low rates of interest.

The white tenant lives adjoining the colored tenant. Their houses are almost equally destitute of comforts. Their living is confined to bare necessities. They are equally burdened with heavy taxes. They pay the same high rent for gullied and impoverished land.

They pay the same enormous prices for farm supplies. Christmas finds them both without any satisfactory return for a year's toil. Dull and heavy and unhappy, they both start the plows again when "New Year's" passes.

Now the People's party says to these two men, "You are kept apart that you may be separately fleeced of your earnings. You are made to hate each other because upon that hatred is rested the keystone of the arch of financial despotism which enslaves you both. You are deceived and blinded that you may not see how this race antagonism perpetuates a monetary system which beggars both."

This is so obviously true it is no wonder both these unhappy laborers stop to listen. No wonder they begin to realize that no change of law can benefit the white tenant which does not benefit the black one likewise; that no system which now does injustice to one of them can fail to injure both. Their every material interest is identical. The moment this becomes a conviction, mere selfishness, the mere desire to better their conditions, escape onerous taxes, avoid usurious charges, lighten their rents, or change their precarious tenements into smiling, happy homes, will drive these two men together, just as their mutually inflamed prejudices now drive them apart.

Suppose these two men now to have become fully imbued with the idea that their material welfare depends upon the reforms we demand. Then they act together to secure them. Every white reformer finds it to the vital interest of his home, his family, his fortune, to see to it that the vote of the colored reformer is freely cast and fairly counted.

Then what? Every colored voter will be thereafter a subject of industrial education and political teaching.

Concede that in the final event, a colored man will vote where his material interests dictate that he should vote; concede that in the South the accident of color can make no possible difference in the interests of farmers, croppers, and laborers; concede that under full and fair discussion the people can be depended upon to ascertain where their interests lie—and we reach the conclusion that the Southern race question can be solved by the People's party on the simple proposition that each race will be led by self-interest to support that which benefits it, when so presented that neither is hindered by the bitter party antagonisms of the past.

Let the colored laborer realize that our platform gives him a better guaranty for political independence; for a fair return for his work; a better chance to buy a home and keep it; a better chance to educate his children and see them profitably employed; a better chance to have public life freed from race collisions; a better chance for every citizen to be considered as a *citizen* regardless of color in the making and enforcing of laws,—let all this be fully realized, and the race question at the South will have settled itself through the evolution of a political movement in which both whites and blacks recognize their surest way out of wretchedness into comfort and independence.

The illustration could be made quite as clearly from other planks in the People's party platform. On questions of land, transportation and finance, especially, the welfare of the two races so clearly depends upon that which benefits either, that intelligent discussion would necessarily lead to just conclusions.

Why should the colored man always be taught that the white man of his neighborhood hates him, while a Northern man, who taxes every rag on his back, loves him? Why should not my tenant come to regard me as his friend rather than the manufacturer who plunders us both? Why should we perpetuate a policy which drives the black man into the arms of the Northern politician?

Why should we always allow Northern and Eastern Democrats to enslave us forever by threats of the Force Bill?

Let us draw the supposed teeth of this fabled dragon by founding our new policy upon justice—upon the simple but profound truth that, if the voice of passion can be hushed, the self-interest of both races will drive them to act in concert. There never was a day during the last twenty years when the South could not have flung the money power into the dust by patiently teaching the Negro that we could not be wretched under any system which would not afflict him likewise; that we could not prosper under any law which would not also bring its blessings to him.

To the emasculated individual who cries "Negro supremacy!" there is little to be said. His cowardice shows him to be a degeneration from the race which has never yet feared any other race. Existing under such conditions as they now do in this country, there is no earthly chance for Negro domination, unless we are ready to admit that the colored man is our superior in will power, courage, and intellect.

Not being prepared to make any such admission in favor of any race the sun ever shone on, I have no words which can portray my contempt for the white men, Anglo-Saxons, who can knock their knees together, and through their chattering teeth and pale lips admit that they are afraid the Negroes will dominate us.

The question of social equality does not enter into the calculation at all. That is a thing each citizen decides for himself. No statute ever yet drew the latch of the humblest home—or ever will. Each citizen regulates his own visiting list—and always will.

The conclusion, then, seems to me to be this: the crushing burdens which now oppress both races in the South will cause each to make an effort to cast them off. They will see a similarity of cause and a similarity of remedy. They will recognize that each should help the other in the work of repealing bad laws and enacting good ones. They will become political allies, and neither can injure the other without weakening both. It will be to the interest of both that each should have justice. And on these broad lines of mutual interest, mutual forbearance, and mutual support the present will be made the stepping stone to future peace and prosperity.

LEWIS HARVIE BLAIR

Lewis Harvie Blair personified the best leadership in the New South. The son of a well-known Old South family, a war-impoverished Confederate veteran who had become one of Virginia's most successful businessmen, Blair, almost alone in his state, stood for the full equality of opportunity and treatment of the Negro. A hardheaded and practical businessman, not an idealist and social reformer, Blair attacked repression of the Negro and all race bigotry on the grounds that they were morally, intellectually, and materially damaging to *all* the South and its people. His appeal was based solely upon the enlightened self-interest of the South, but among his fellow Virginians and the rest of the white South it fell upon deaf ears.

In late 1893, when the following essay appeared in *Our Day,* Blair was already Virginia's best-known heretic—a foe of worship of the past, an advocate of free trade, and the author of *The Prosperity of the South Dependent Upon the Elevation of the Negro.* It was this fame which had led to an invitation to deliver an address before the African Congress held at the Columbian Exposition in Chicago in 1893. Blair prepared the essay reprinted here, but the financial crisis of that year prevented his absence from business affairs long enough for him to deliver it in person, so it was read for him.

For another five years, at least, Blair continued to berate complacent Virginians, while the state's leaders with increasing tempo moved toward outright disfranchisement and complete segregation of the Negro. Then, sometime between 1898 and 1915,

Blair completely reversed himself and declared, "The only logical position for the Negro is complete subordination to the whites." Other liberal views he continued to hold until his death in 1916. He heartily approved of the progressive reforms of the Wilson administration and even advocated establishment of a form of socialism which he called "state paternalism." He had become a typical Southern Progressive—Progressivism was for white men only.

Both Blair and Tom Watson, in the tragedy of their reaction, ironically share with two American Negroes the bitter price exacted of men who once hopefully wrestled with the "Negro Problem": Richard Wright, the native son who died embittered, disillusioned, an expatriate in France, and William Edward Burghardt Du Bois, the fiery yet scholarly and poetic man who rests today in the soil of Ghana, the Africa from which his people sprang.

The
Southern Problem
and its Solution

BRIEFLY stated and divested of sophistry, the Southern Problem is the settled determination of the whites to ignore the civil and political equality of the Negroes, to deprive them of natural and constitutional rights and to keep them in absolute subjection—in a word, to suppress the Negro as a man and citizen. Kindness, consideration, generosity, and even strict equity from individual whites to individual Negroes do not negative this statement of the problem, because collectively, the whites at the cry of "Nigger" immediately band themselves into solid phalanx to oppose every move or measure looking to equality of citizenship, regardless of race or color, but they visit with political death and social disability all who advocate or even believe that the principle on which our government is founded, namely, the equality of all men, shall be a vital reality and not a barren ideality.*

To state the Southern Problem is, however, easier than to find or rather to apply the solution after discovered. The solution is simply, to do right, to exact no more than is just, and to be willing to do to others as we have a right to be done by. But what is right is so often beclouded by ignorance, prejudice and selfishness, it is ofttimes not only difficult to know the right, but, especially when enjoying unrighteous advantages, more difficult to be willing to do right after right is plainly acknowledged. Now the Southern Problem, like perhaps all great moral and social problems, is thus beclouded, and it is mainly a conflict between right and knowledge on one side and

*Reprinted from *Our Day,* XII (November, 1893), 361–76.

selfishness and ignorance on the other, complicated, however, by a large admixture of an inferior race, but for which admixture there would be no Southern Problem. But with this admixture, introducing race antipathy and the fear that unless the inferior race is arbitrarily suppressed, it may, directly or by combination, gain control and upset social order, the problem becomes so difficult it is doubtful whether human nature is equal to the solution. But whether equal or not, we should not be deterred by difficulties however grave, and each good citizen should do what in him lies to solve a problem which has already immensely impaired the welfare and happiness of the South, and which threatens if unsolved to plunge her into a condition, moral, material and intellectual, little superior to Mexico or the South American republics.

No one man, however great, is sufficient, but all may assist. As proudest structure is built of innumerable little bricks, each insignificant in itself, so the Southern Problem may be solved by innumerable little acts or suggestions, each insignificant in itself. I now therefore cast my two mites into the treasury whence solution may flow, thankful if they tend in the least to the solution of a problem upon which depend the welfare and happiness of the millions now inhabiting the South, and of the untold millions yet to inhabit it.

The South herself must solve her problem. Others may, indeed must assist and encourage, but the South must work out her own solution. The South may be anathematized for her treatment of her black children, and the anathemas may be richly merited, but they will only confirm her in her treatment—like fabled traveler exposed to wintry blasts, she will hug her delusions only the closer. The South may be approached on her sentimental, on her humanitarian, on her religious side, and the appeals may be ever so eloquent and pathetic but they will all be in vain, because human nature while enjoying unjust gains and privileges, has never yet heeded such appeals. Human nature must first be convinced that unjust dealings mean material injury, and that just dealings mean material good; must be convinced that tyranny and oppression, though first blighting the oppressed finally blight the oppressor, and leave the state a desolate barbarism.

Now the South is enjoying unjust gains, privileges and advantages, at the expense of six millions of its fellow citizens, and it ignorantly supposes that this condition of affairs is for her benefit, and so long as the South so believes, she cannot be expected to take any steps to alter existing conditions. Hence to induce the South to recognize a Southern Problem and then to solve it, the South must be convinced that her settled determination to deprive the Negroes of their natural and constitutional rights, and to keep them in subjection really worse than slavery, destroys her prosperity, saps her political strength, and endangers if not dooms her peculiar civilization which she cherishes so fondly.

How, then, can the South be convinced? By appeals to her intelligent self-interest, and there are many avenues by which she can be approached. Ah! but that is so low, so degrading a motive! Possibly; but it is the only lever available in the present condition of human nature. But such motive is not low and degrading for the argument of good *sometime* or *somewhere* is the only motive that can permanently influence men, however exalted. But whether exalted or degraded, appeal to intelligent self-interest is the contribution I now bring to the solution of the Southern Problem.

Returning to our starting point, the Southern Problem is this: The South believes that the Negro must be suppressed, otherwise he may, directly or indirectly, gain control. In that event, not only prosperity but civilization will be destroyed. Therefore, to prevent such dire results, the Negro must be deprived of his natural and constitutional rights. The result of such belief is what I shall call coercion.

Coercion then is the position to be turned, the citadel to be captured, and the way to turn or capture is to test coercion by its fruits. If its fruits are good, they will be revealed by the prosperity and happiness of the South; if bad, they will be revealed by the bad condition of the South. The conflict must rage around

the good or bad fruits of coercion. Now, nobody claims the South
to be either prosperous or satisfied. It may therefore be affirmed
that the fruits of coercion are not good. But now show that its
fruits are not only bad, but destructive—first destroying prosperity,
and second, civilization, because no, certainly no high, civilization
can long exist apart from prosperity. If this is done successfully the
South may probably be convinced of the evils of coercion, which
may then be abandoned, and the Southern Problem is solved. To
convince the South, approach it somewhat as follows:

For the past eighteen years you have with incessant vigilance
and an iron hand, so coerced the Negroes and all suspected of
a desire to accord them the full or even qualified rights of citizens,
that not a voice from Potomac to Mississippi is lifted in opposition.
This is long enough to test the merits of coercion. Now what are
its merits? To test them show the condition of affairs individually
and collectively; and first, What is the condition of the individual?
Inquiry will elicit the reply, Bad, very bad; that outside of a few
cities few are prospering, most are ever struggling to keep head
above water, and many are bankrupt; that values have steadily
depreciated; that all are sellers, but that their improved estates that
twenty years ago sold readily at ten or more dollars an acre, are
now unsaleable at price of wild government land; that their crops
have dwindled, their barns have decayed, their fences have rotted,
their orchards have died, their ditches have clogged, their fields
have returned to nature, and their cattle have diminished; that
discontent vexes and despondency oppresses, and that people are
deserting birthplace and heritage, and flying to cities or to states
where, coercion being unknown, prosperity prevails.

As proving abandonment of home, show by census that between
1880 and 1890 forty percent of the natural increase of the nine
Southern states east of the Mississippi, and sixty percent of the
natural increase of Virginia fled the land of their birth. Such is the
lamentable condition of the whites. The condition of the Negroes—
their indigence and consequently their ignorance and degradation,
are beyond description. Drive home these and other evil effects of
coercion, and if the South will not listen to the logic and eloquence

of facts, neither will she be persuaded though Washington himself arose from the dead. Solution will then be hopeless.

Second, show how coercion injuries the Commonwealth, and to do this compare the nine Cis-Mississippi Southern states with the five states of Minnesota, Nebraska, Kansas, and the Dakotas, beginning with 1880 when coercion was fully developed. Both groups are agricultural with the advantage in 1880 on the side of the South, which by reason of great abundance of cheap lands, virgin and improved, presented the advantages of new states and by reason of long settlement, the advantage of old states. If therefore coercion has been good, the South should at least compare favorably with the five Western states in growth of population, cities, productions and political weight. Show from the fourteenth number of the Statistical Abstract of the United States their growth in these respects.

GROWTH OF POPULATION FROM 1880 TO 1890.

South, nine states.	West, five states.
1,746,601 16½ percent.	1,934,917 82 percent.

Southern growth from 1800 to 1860 averaged about thirty percent each decade. Losing thus in ten years under coercion forty percent of its natural increase, is strong condemnation of coercion.

GROWTH OF CITIES OF TEN THOUSAND AND UPWARD, 1880 TO 1890.

South, thirty-five cities.	West, sixteen cities.
352,177 45 percent.	521,116 245 percent.

Growth of cities is best indication of growth of wealth. Under non-coercion wealth has increased faster by fivefold than under coercion—a heavy verdict against coercion.

GROWTH OF LIVESTOCK AND CEREALS.   1880 TO 1890.

	South, nine states		West, five states.	
Livestock	1,034,470	5 percent.	12,321,880	145 percent.
Wheat	3,100,000	12 percent.	136,350,000	185 percent.
Corn	60,600,000	25 percent.	167,000,000	90 percent.

A mere nominal increase; a large relative decrease. This is not because the South needed little of such things, for she imports yearly millions of dollars worth of meats, lard, butter, cheese, bread and forage, but because coercion, as will be shown later, necessarily diverts attention and energies from the profitable pursuit of agriculture to the barren pursuit of politics.

GROWTH OF REPRESENTATION.   1880 TO 1890.

South, nine states.	West, five states.
2 3 percent.	9 60 percent.

GROWTH OF OTHER SOUTHERN PRODUCTS.   1880 TO 1890.

Nine states.		
Cotton (Bales)	978,913	23 percent.
Tobacco (Lbs.)	11,000,000	9 percent.
Sugar (Tons)	99,716	79 percent.

Now why this pitiful increase of crops distinctively Southern, even its boasted crop, cotton, increasing only twenty-three percent. It is not for lack of natural advantages, because the South, with its fine climate, fertile soil, and unlimited virgin acres, yields with little effort earth's choicest fruits. It is not because of people, for they are pure English, partially crossed with best Scotch and Huguenot blood, are hospitable, generous, and chivalrous, and are equal on occasion, to great deeds and noble thoughts. Lacking then, neither conditions nor people, why her nominal growth but relative decay?

The reason is plain, coercion or denial of natural and constitutional rights has done the damaging work. For to coerce successfully as the South has done absorbs the energies and faculties and leaves neither leisure nor inclination for beneficent industry. The South, therefore, having devoted herself to political instead of material ends, to suppress and repress six of its fifteen million citizens instead of to create values, it was inevitable that the South should fail to prosper and progress, and should suffer political decay. On the other hand the five Western states have flourished wonderfully and gained political weight because they had no political orthodoxy, no arbitrary standard to which all, under heavy penalty, must conform; because men were permitted and encouraged to view social and political matters from every standpoint and to speak their minds accordingly. Not what one believed but what one did was their touchstone, and consideration came not from opinions but works show also that if the people had been compelled to occupy one identical standpoint and to inherit their opinions as rigidly as their names, there could have been no progress, and their fertile prairies would still have been wilds cropped by buffaloes, with trappers and Indians their sole inhabitants. Show the South that if she wishes to prosper she must imitate; must uncage thought and free the tongue, and must urge her sons to discard proscription and intolerance. Freedom of opinion and discussion has never yet injured any good cause, and it will not injure but promote the best interests of the South.

Show that coercion injuries morally—because coercion is tryanny or trampling upon rights, and neither individual nor state can deliberately and persistently do this without degrading the sense of right; because trampling on Negroes' rights inevitably leads to trampling on whites' rights, and despising Negroes' lives to despising whites' lives—leads to the reign of the murderous revolver when differences though trivial, are settled not by right or reason, but by the quickest shooter—leads to the frequent murders, homicides and assassinations among the whites themselves. Show that from disregard of life and rights in their humblest form, to disregard in their highest forms, the path is direct, and that soon no life is sacred but is sacrificed without justification, compunction, or redress.

Intellectually—because coercion requires the South to be, on constant guard lest the coerced successfully assert their rights, and to devote time, thought and energy to making the coerced stay coerced. The South has therefore neither taste nor leisure for intellectual pursuits, for little except for ignoble politics or the art, right or wrong, of keeping atop and enjoying the honors, emoluments and immunities of the state. The stump becomes the intellectual school of the South.

Materially—because coercion, demanding and engrossing attention, leaves little time or energy for industrial pursuits; because coercion, trampling upon the rights of Negroes destroys their hope and ambition, and having no stimulus to exertion and improvement they naturally remain unprofitable, impairing instead of promoting public welfare. Press points like these and show in addition that the deplorable degradation of the Negroes reacts fearfully upon the lower ranks of whites, making and keeping them also degraded and unprofitable. Many think that degrading Negroes elevates whites and that elevating Negroes degrades whites; but show that this is a fatal error because whites and Negroes are in the same boat, not separate, and because their fortunes are inextricably linked, rising and falling together, not alternately.

Show the South that her interest lies in enfranchising not coercing the Negroes, in inviting, not repelling their cooperation; in encouraging them to vote and participate in public affairs; in making them feel that they have a country and are not despised aliens in their native land, and that they have rights inalienable and not with a string to them and the string in our hands. Show that ten percent increase in earning capacity of our 6,118,592 Negroes, now as a body non-self-supporting, would make its happy influence felt in our own households from Potomac to Rio Grande: that an increase of twenty-five per cent would mean general prosperity and happiness, and that an increase to the normal earning capacity of whites elsewhere would mean the South's complete restoration, moral, material, intellectual, and political—all sacrificed to coercion.

Show that coercion expatriates the flower of the youth. First, because coercion is intolerance, and coercion can be successfully sustained only by rigid suppression of independence, and ambitious youth, rather than submit, seeks other regions where speech and action are untrammeled, and where sentiment and intellect find free expression and full expansion. Such youth, the flower of any community, wither in an atmosphere of repression, and they must expatriate themselves or perish, and they have expatriated themselves by thousands, to enduring loss of native and lasting gain of adopted states. Law, medicine and politics excepted, eminent Southerners are not found in land of birth, reflecting luster thereon, but North, East, West, where independence is encouraged and honored, and intolerance dishonored and discouraged. Coercion, expatriation, ruin on the one hand; liberty, non-expatriation, prosperity on the other show the South that it must choose one or the other.

Second, because coercion, as will be seen, restricts the growth of manufactures. Consequently there is little home employment for skilled and educated youth, and they must seek occupation elsewhere or starve. The Southerner who educates a son for manufacturing, mechanical or scientific pursuits soon finds that son, if half worth the cost of his education, as effectively expatriated as if sentence of banishment had been decreed against him. Its inevitable fruit, expatriation of the flower of the youth, is strongest condemnation of coercion.

Manufactures are power: the secret of Great Britain's universal and of New England's and Pennsylvania's national supremacy, is manufactures. Manufactures are wealth: the enormous wealth of England and the scarcely less enormous wealth of Massachusetts and the middle states is due to manufactures. Show the South, however, that she can enjoy neither wealth nor power under coercion, because coercion requires time, thought and energy to be devoted to suppression instead of expansion, and to be diverted from industrial to political pursuits; coercion is therefore fatal to manufactures. With mind, heart and soul engrossed in suppressing the natural, and in invalidating the legal, rights of forty percent of its population, manufactures have little show. Hence it is not surprising that according to census of 1890 the manufactures of eight principal southern cities with a population of 586,292 amounted to only $111,605,000. Cincinnati, with half their population (296,908) manufactured sixty percent more, or $178,650,000. Coercion is fatal to manufactures, and if the South wishes to enjoy manufactures with their attendant wealth, power and happiness, she must sacrifice coercion.

The South longs for immigration with an eager but mortifying longing. Show, however, that immigrants will not come so long as coercion stands like a lion to repel; that while fleeing the coercion of an old, immigration will shun the coercion of a new country. Show that immigration demands freedom and quiet, and that neither cheap and fertile soil nor fine climate will attract if coupled with intolerance, or if violence prevails or is even apprehended. Show that without a complete surrender of coercion, with its intolerance, intimidation and violence, the South can never enjoy the stimulating and lifegiving influences of immigration. Plead she never so earnestly, and offer she never so great advantages, all will be neutralized so long as the South worships at the shrine of coercion.

Show that coercion is the parent of the deeds of violence that damage and discredit the South. Coercion is trampling upon rights, and because the South ignores the rights and despises the lives of Negroes, general disregard of rights and lives is begotten, and hence, impatient of the restraints of law and reason, wrongs, real or imaginary, are redressed offhand, and the press bristles with accounts not only of lynchings and slayings of Negroes, but of affrays, homicides, murders and assassinations among the whites. Hence, also, the carrying of revolvers, one never knowing when for some trivial difference he may be called upon to defend his own or seek his neighbor's life. That this is not fancy nor misrepresentation but truth, may be abundantly proved by such summaries as the following from two issues of the Richmond, *Dispatch,* and by editorial of Charleston *News and Courier:*

Richmond *Dispatch,* July 7, 1892. Two men slain; one badly shot by brother-in-law; one assassination; one on trial for assassination; one negro lynched and another negro sought for lynching. This in Virginia, supposed to be law-abiding. Two negroes lynched in Vicksburg, one in Clay County, Ala., and one Benson slain in Birmingham.

July 21, 1892. Chief of Police, Montgomery, W. Virginia, slain; one Wyatt, single-handed hangs a negro; one, Talt Hall, to be returned to Wise C. H., Va., for resentence to death; one, Taylor, murderer of whole Mullins family captured; one, Smith, tried in Roanoke, Va., for aggravated murder; Governor of Virginia offers reward for capture of three murderers; three affrays in one day in Windsor, N. C." Charleston *News and Courier,* June 16th, 1892. A Murderous Record. The killing of Alderman Gilreath of Greenville, by J. M. Sullivan, adds another to the rapidly-lengthening roll of murders in our blood-drenched State, and, according to report, was committed without a shadow of justification. The circumstances as narrated by our correspondent, show that Sullivan deliberately shot an unarmed man, who was standing still and making no demonstration or even threat of violence, and after thus inflicting a mortal would on him shot him in the back, inflicting another.

We do not mention these circumstances for the purpose of commenting on this particular crime. Deplorable as it is, it is one of hundreds of similar recent occurrences, and comment on them appears to be wasted. We do not refrain, however, from influencing the jury. We take for granted that Mr. Sullivan will be acquitted as hundreds of men of his position in the State have been acquitted before him, and as many men no doubt will be acquitted after him, this year and next and thereafter. The slaughter is going on steadily, and there appears to be little or no hope of stopping it.

What we wish to direct the attention of the people to particularly is one feature of most of these crimes which is so sharply emphasized by the murder of Mr. Gilreath. That feature is their unprovoked and cowardly character.

Week after week, and sometimes day by day, reports are published of the death or deadly wounding of men who have committed no offense that would warrant even an angry blow from their slayers. It was so in this Greenville case; it is so in more than half the cases reported; we believe it is safe to say that the assertion holds true of nine cases of homicide in the state in ten. The men who are killed among us now are killed without cause.

And not only are the killings unprovoked and unjustifiable in the greater number of instances. They are as cowardly in character as they are unprovoked. It is rarely—so rarely that out of all the number of killings reported in recent years we cannot recall a single instance— that we hear of a man being killed in a fair fight or in a fight of any kind. The slayer usually comes off without a scratch. The rule is that he shoots his victim without warning, without giving him a chance to defend himself, and excuses his crime in the courthouse to a jury of his 'peers'—save the mark!—by the plea that his victim 'made a motion as if to draw a pistol.'

It is a familiar pretext and a successful one, the only drawback to

its merit being, indeed, that the victim is usually found not to have
had a pistol and it is to be assumed that he would not have pretended
to have had one in his circumstances. The dead are dumb, however,
and the murderer tells the story for both—he acted strictly on the
defensive. There have not been, we believe, a dozen homicides in
South Carolina since the war, in which the slayer was a white man,
that the plea was not made and allowed that the unarmed man who
was killed was acting on the offensive, and the man with the revolver
was protecting himself from violence.

These things tell their own story—and it is told in blood. The number of killings is multiplying instead of diminishing, and as we have
pointed out, they are becoming more murderous, more cold-blooded in
character. Men kill whom they please with as little compunction as they
would kill a dog, and with but little more risk to themselves. It is
a hard saying, but it is true.

We need not shut our eyes or our mouths to our condition; it is
known of all men, and they avoid our soil as they would a desert.
We must work a change somehow and soon, or it will be worse than
a desert.

The editor, however, misses the point of these deeds of blood
among the whites, which is this: Negroes' lives are thoroughly
despised in South Carolina and the South, and it is as already
stated, but a step from despising and sacrificing black to despising
and sacrificing white life. Respect for black life must be inspired
before deeds of blood among the whites will cease. Show that
until violence, no matter by whom or against whom committed,
is sternly punished, that until law is respected and life safe, growth,
prosperity, civilization itself, are impossible.

Show that of all forms of violence engendered by coercion the
most damaging and demoralizing, because the most unnecessary
and indefensible, are the constant lynchings of Negroes.

Show that lynching Negroes is doubly inexcusable because there
is no danger of guilty Negroes' escape, for the reason that the
superior the world over, however tender of his blood when ar-
raigned, is as prodigal of inferior's blood, as when, for instance,
at Laurens, S. C., in September, 1891, ten Negroes were sentenced
to death for shedding, not superior's but inferior's blood, which

GEORGE WASHINGTON CABLE

From C. Vann Woodward, *Tom Watson, Agrarian Rebel* (Macmillan)

THOMAS E. WATSON

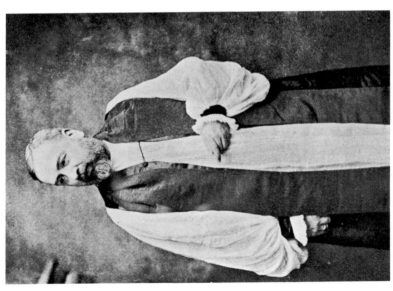

THOMAS U. DUDLEY

LEWIS HARVIE BLAIR

ANDREW SLEDD

JOHN SPENCER BASSETT

QUINCY EWING

at best is valued so lightly. Show that Negroes are lynched not only for alleged assault, but on any and every pretext, even for petty theft. Thus the Charleston *News and Courier* of June 10th, 1892, editorially commenting on the official report of the prosecuting attorney "that Dave Shaw was brutally murdered" says, "It is to be hoped that its discovery will soon relieve the State of the shame and reproach of the latest crime charged to the account of its citizens—the lynching of a (negro) man for petty theft." Also in summary already given from Richmond *Dispatch*, July 7th, 1892, two Negroes were lynched at Vicksburg for alleged homicide: in summary of July 21st, one man, single-handed swung up a Negro for alleged theft, and the same paper of August 21st, 1891, reports two women lynched near Montgomery, Ala., for alleged arson. These are only samples of what the press constantly reports. Show also by extracts like this from editorial of Louisville *Christian Observer* of March 1st, 1893, the frightful increase of these frightful deeds of violence: "In the year 1883 there were thirty-nine cases of lynchings and none of punishment. Accordingly in 1884 there was an increase to fifty-three cases. Still no punishment. In 1888, seventy-two; in 1889, ninety-five; in 1890, one hundred; in 1891, one hundred and sixty-nine; in 1892, two hundred and thirty-six cases. If we let this evil continue growing and at such a ratio, how long before the security of life will be destroyed?"

But so long as coercion is popular, lynchings, horrible and injurious as they are, will be popular.

Though the South must solve its own problem, yet others, as already said, must assist, and the others are the North. They must not only preach equity for the blacks, they must also act equity. An ounce of acted equity is worth a pound of preached equity, or an hundred-weight of denounced iniquity. Its many Negroes make the race problem a difficult one for the South under the most favorable circumstances. The South, therefore, is not wholly blamable for displaying towards the Negro much of the dark side of human nature. The small number of Negroes North, however, reduces its race problem to zero, and makes their discrimination against them wholly inexcusable. Yet notwithstanding its slight temptation, the North treats its few Negroes with much injustice. Thus in great, cosmopolitan New York, where if anywhere, impartiality might be expected, the Negro may not satisfy hunger at best hotel, may not quench thirst at leading saloon, may not gratify taste at select opera, may not even bind up broken heart at fashionable church. He may join neither lodge, union, post, club, guild nor exchange; may follow neither trades nor mechanic arts, may drive neither public cab nor public truck; may not even dig the public streets, may follow only degrading, menial and ill-paid pursuits—his welfare hindered and his manhood affronted everywhere, or with rare exceptions. He is never safe from insult and even violence, and his wrongs generally await redress till the great assize where all wrongs are supposed to be righted and all wrong doers punished. The mob too, sometimes (Port Jarvis, N.Y., June 1st, 1892, and other instances) seizes him for sacrifice and outraged justice folds her hands in her helplessness or indifference.

Now if the North desires the Southern Problem solved, it must clear its skirts of the stain of injustice towards its helpless blacks. Injustice is excusable nowhere and to nobody, but if the South is inexcusable the North is triply inexcusable, because the natural temptation to oppress the inferior race is ever-present and ever strong with the South, while with the North such natural temptation scarcely exists. So long, therefore, as injustice to Negroes, whether positive, such as violence, or negative, such as denial or curtail of natural rights, prevails North, solution is well-nigh impossible, because one wrong North will be made to justify thousands South, one act of violence North be made to justify thousands South and one lynching North to justify innumerable lynchings South. A heavy responsibility, therefore, rests upon the North whose temptations are few, to treat the Negro not only justly but generously, not only to place no impediments in, but to take them out of his path; not only coldly to leave him to work out his own salvation but to extend a fraternal, helping, sympathetic hand.

When the North thus acts, it may then, because its hands will be clean, with hope appeal to the South to do likewise, but until the North does so act, the most eloquent, fervent, pathetic appeals will be regarded as impertinence, and will be met by the old but still effective reply, "Physician, heal thyself."

This is not the solution of the Southern Problem. It is only a slight contribution tending to solution: a few suggestions showing how the question should be approached and handled. I merely design to strike the keynote: its thousands of variations may be applied and supplied, each for himself. Solution must be the combined result of innumerable efforts, each insignificant perhaps in itself, and of indefinite time—fifty, sixty years, perhaps never.

But the only likely method of solution is by appeal to intelligent self-interest.

ANDREW SLEDD

Andrew Sledd, like his father, was a Methodist minister. Born into an old Virginia family in Lynchburg in 1870, he received both the B.A. and M.A. degrees from Randolph-Macon College, and an A.M. degree from Harvard. He taught school in Arkansas and Virginia, and in 1898 was appointed professor of Latin at Emory College in tiny, rural Oxford, Georgia. It was from there he dared to write that the South's treatment of the Negro was wrong and that the Negro, too, possessed inalienable rights. He bitterly denounced the barbarity of lynching, the blame for which he laid to all the white South, since the better elements rarely bestirred themselves to prevent it. Sledd declared, concerning those who usually perpetrated the actual lynching: "Our lower classes must be *made* to realize, by whatever means, that the black man has rights which they are *bound* to respect."

This indictment appeared in the July, 1902, issue of the *Atlantic Monthly,* a journal which few Georgians read, and, perhaps for that reason, the expected reaction was slow to come. But when it did, there were none to defend the principles of free speech, academic freedom, or even justice. Emory was in those days a small, poor Methodist college, and since Sledd was a minister in the church, as well as a professor at Emory, his position and the principle of academic freedom were not as strong as those of John Spencer Bassett and Trinity College when Bassett committed a similar transgression the next year. The result was that Sledd submitted his resignation, which was eagerly accepted by the president and board of trustees.

The most that Sledd's colleagues at Emory would do for him was to persuade the trustees to appropriate a thousand dollars to finance his work toward a doctoral degree at Yale University. Receiving the degree in 1903, Sledd returned to the South, first to Southern University (now Birmingham-Southern College) as professor of Greek, and then to the new University of Florida as its first president. After four years he was forced out of this position, because the student body had not grown beyond forty-seven students, while there were twenty-two faculty members. He then returned to Southern University and served as its president until 1914, when he rejoined Emory at its new location in Atlanta. On the faculty of Emory's Candler School of Theology he gained a national reputation as a Biblical scholar, but he never again became embroiled in the race issue.

Unlike Cable, who permanently left the South, and unlike both Watson and Blair, who later renounced their liberal views on race, Sledd not only stayed in the South, but, according to a recent scholar, held to his liberal views until death, in 1939.

The Negro:
Another View

So much has appeared in the public prints touching the various phases of the Negro problem in the South that it is perhaps presumptuous to attempt any further contribution to the literature on that subject. Previous discussion, however, seems open to two very serious criticisms,—it has been largely *sectional;* and, by consequence, it has been for the most part *partisan.**

Northern writers, with practically no knowledge or experience of actual conditions, have theorized to meet a condition that they did not understand. Since emancipation, the Negro has been regarded as the rightful protégé of the section that wrought his freedom; and his cause has been championed with a bitter and undiscriminating zeal as earnest as it is misguided. Southern writers, on the contrary, remembering the Negro as the slave, consider him and his rights from a position of proud and contemptuous superiority, and would deal with him on the antebellum basis of his servile state.

The North, with many things in the Southern treatment of the Negro justly open to impeachment, by a general indictment at once weakens its own case and fortifies the evils it seeks to overthrow. The South, in answer to what is unjust in the charge of the North, recalls former days, persuades herself of the righteousness of her cause, and continually recommits herself to an antiquated and unsound policy.

Such partisan and sectional discussion cannot fail to be alike bitter and unfruitful. While it may, indeed, have been natural at

*Reprinted from *Atlantic Monthly*, XC (July, 1902), 65–73.

the close of the Civil War that the hostile sections should align themselves on opposite sides, and carry on by the pen, and with a more virulent because impotent animosity, the discussion that had been fought out with the sword, yet now, surely, the time for such recrimination is past. If we are, indeed, one people, *United* States in more than name only, the problems, perplexities, and interests of every section appertain in no slight or trivial measure to the country as a whole. It is true that each section and state and county and township has its own problems—but the particular problems of the part are the general problems of the whole; and the nation, as a nation, is interested in the administration and concerns of the most insignificant members of the body politic.

It would be trite and old fashioned to apply to ourselves the old fable of the body and its members; but we surely lie open to its application in our treatment of the Negro question. The South has regarded it as a local and not a national matter; has refused to receive any light upon it from outside sources; and has met any suggestions and offers of outside help with a surly invitation to "mind your own business." The North, on the other hand, considering the question in its wider bearings, has approached it from the side of preformed theories, rather than of actual facts; in a spirit of tearful or indignant sentimentality, rather than of calm, unbiased reason; and has therefore proposed remedies that must, in the very nature of things, be at once undesirable and impossible. As is usual in such cases, the truth lies between the two extremes.

The Negro question is a national one; as much so as the question of tariff, of immigration, of subsidies, or any such issue that is universally recognized as touching the interests of the whole people. It is but right, therefore, that the solution of the question should command the attention and enlist the interest of the people as a people, regardless of section or party or antebellum attitude; and the South has no right to take offense at any well-meant and kindly effort to relieve the situation.

But, at the same time, the fact must be recognized that the Negro question is not different from all other questions, does not occupy a place apart, unique, and cannot be dealt with in any other way than the common, rational method applicable to the commonest social and political problem. Ignorance of the facts cannot take the place of knowledge here any more than elsewhere. Sentiment cannot safely here or elsewhere usurp the place of reason. Blindness, prejudice, uncharitableness, vilification, have the same value here as elsewhere, and are as likely to lead to a fair and satisfactory solution of the Negro problem as of any other —just as likely and no more. We must, as a whole people, candidly and honestly recognize a certain set of underlying facts, which may or may not differ from our theories, cross our sympathies, or contravene our wishes. Then we shall be in a position to deal with the question.

Now, the fundamental facts to be recognized in the case are these:

1. *The Negro belongs to an inferior race.*

And this not by reason of any previous condition of servitude or brutal repression on the part of his former master, whether in the days of slavery or since; not on account of his color or his past or present poverty, ignorance, and degradation. These, to be sure, must be reckoned with; but they do not touch the fundamental proposition.

The Negro is lower in the scale of development than the white man. His inferiority is radical and inherent, a physiological and racial inequality that may, indeed, be modified by environment, but cannot be erased without the indefinite continuance of favorable surroundings and the lapse of indefinite time. But what the Negro race may become in the remote future by process of development and selection is not a matter for present consideration. The fact remains that now the Negro race is an inferior race.

There can hardly be any need to defend this proposition in these days of the boasted universal supremacy of the Anglo-Saxon. Occasionally we hear hysterical utterances by Negroes or by well-meaning, but misguided friends of the race to the effect that the Negro is the equal of any white man anywhere. But in general such ill-advised cant is being laid aside, and the inferiority of the race is coming to be recognized.

This is a hopeful sign. And the general recognition of the proper place of the freedman will go far toward adjusting conflicting theories and removing lingering sectional misunderstanding and bitterness. It will do away at once with all those schemes that used to find favor in the North, and are still at times most unwisely advocated, for the establishment of social equality and the amalgamation of the races.

Probably no scheme advanced for the solution of this problem has given more lasting offense to the people of the South, or done more to embitter sectional feeling than this of amalgamation. It has been received in the same spirit, and has engendered the same feelings, as a proposition to bring about equality and a union between some cultured New England belle and the public scavenger of her city, with all the filth and foulness of his calling on his person and in his blood. The very words are sickening. And the idea, so coarse and repugnant to every finer feeling, could have originated only in the brain of the wildest theorist, ignorant of conditions, and hurried by his Negrophile propensities and desire to do justice to the black man into entire forgetfulness of the rights and feelings of the Southern white man.

There seems to be no essential condition of causality between the previous bondage and suffering of the Negro and the assumption by him or for him, on emancipation, of any equality with his former master other than the grand and fundamental equality of man to man before God and the national law. Emancipation could not eradicate the essential inferiority of the Negro. No such conditions existed as in other states of slavery—in Greece or Rome, for example, where the slave was often of kindred blood, and even higher born, better educated, and of finer tastes and feelings than his master. Emancipation there might naturally be followed by an approximate equality between the ex-slave and his former master. But the Negro when enslaved was—a Negro; and the emancipated Negro was a Negro still. Freedom had not made him a new creature. He was, indeed, better than when he entered slavery; but his emancipation had not changed, and could not change, the fundamental features, the natural inferiority of his race.

2. *But the Negro has inalienable rights.*

While the North has erred in approaching the Negro question with the assertion of the equality of the races, and seeking to solve it on that unsound postulate, the South has, much more grievously, erred in precisely the opposite direction. For our section has carried the idea of the Negro's inferiority almost, if not quite, to the point of dehumanizing him. This is an unpalatable truth; but that it is the truth, few intelligent and candid white men, even of the South, would care to deny. Blatant demagogues, political shysters, courting favor with the mob; news sheets, flattering the prejudices, and pandering to the passions of their constituency; ignorant youths and loud-voiced men who receive their information at second hand, and either do not or cannot see—these, and their followers, assert with frothing vehemence that the Negro is fairly and kindly treated in the South, that the Southern white man is the Negro's friend, and gives him even more than his just desert.

But, if we care to investigate, evidences of our brutal estimate of the black man are not far to seek. The hardest to define is perhaps the most impressive—the general tacit attitude and feeling of the average Southern community toward the Negro. He is either nothing more than the beast that perishes, unnoticed and uncared for so long as he goes quietly about his menial toil (as a young man recently said to the writer, "The farmer regards his nigger in the same light as his mule," but this puts the matter far too favorably for the Negro); or, if he happens to offend, he is punished as a beast with a curse or a kick, and with tortures that even the beast is spared; or, if he is thought of at all in a general way, it is with the most absolute loathing and contempt. He is either unnoticed or despised. As for his feelings, he hasn't any. How few—alas how few—words of gentleness and courtesy ever come to the black man's ear! But harsh and imperious words, coarseness and cursing, how they come upon him, whether with excuse or in the frenzy of unjust and unreasoning passion! And his rights of person, property, and sanctity of home—who ever heard of the "rights" of a "nigger"? This is the general sentiment, in the air, intangible, but strongly felt; and it is, in a large measure, this sentiment that creates and perpetuates the Negro problem.

If the Negro could be made to feel that his *fundamental* rights and privileges are recognized and respected equally with those of the white man, that he is not discriminated against both publicly and privately simply and solely because of his color, that he is regarded and dealt with as a responsible, if humble, member of society, the most perplexing features of his problem would be at once simplified, and would shortly, in normal course, disappear. But the Negro cannot entertain such feelings while the evidence of their groundlessness and folly is constantly thrust upon him. We do not now speak of the utterly worthless and depraved. There are many such; but we whose skins are white need to remember that our color too has its numbers of the ignorant, lecherous, and wholly bad. But take a good Negro—well educated, courteous, God-fearing. There are many such; and they are, in everything save color, superior to many white men. But what is their life? As they walk our streets, they lift their hats in passing the aged or the prominent, whether man or woman; yet no man so returns their salutation. They would go away; at the depot they may not enter the room of the whites, and on the train they must occupy their own separate and second-class car. Reaching their destination, they may not eat at the restaurant of the whites, or rest at the white hotel. If they make purchases, shop ladies and messenger gentlemen look down upon them with manifest contempt, and treat them with open brusqueness and contumely. And if, on a Sabbath, they would worship in a white man's church, they are bidden to call upon God, the maker of the black man as well as of the white, and invoke the Christ, who died for black and white alike, from a place apart. And so, from the cradle to the grave, the Negro is made, in Southern phrase, "to know and keep his place."

In the case we are considering, these distinctions are not based on this Negro's ignorance, on his viciousness, on his offensiveness of person or of manner; for he is educated, good, cleanly, and courteous. They are based solely on the fact that he is a Negro. They do not so operate in the case of a white man. But the black man, *because of his blackness,* is put in this lowest place in public esteem and treatment.

Lynching, again, is but a more inflamed and conspicuous expression of this same general sentiment. An investigation of the statistics of this practice in the United States will bring to light several interesting and startling facts.

1. In the last decade of the last century of Christian grace and civilization, more men met their death by violence at the hands of lynchers than were executed by due process of law. And this holds true, with possibly one exception, for each year in the decade. The total number thus hurried untried and unshriven into eternity during these ten unholy years approximated seventeen hundred souls.

2. The lynching habit is largely sectional. Seventy to eighty percent of all these lynchings occur in the Southern states.

3. The lynchings are largely racial. About three quarters of those thus done to death are Negroes.

4. The lynching penalty does not attend any single particular crime, which, by its peculiar nature and heinousness, seems to demand such violent and lawless punishment. But murder, rape, arson, barn burning, theft—or suspicion of any of these—may and do furnish the ground for mob violence.

These facts, especially the second, third, and fourth items, are bitterly controverted in the section which they most concern. But they are as demonstrable as any other facts, and demand the assent of every candid mind.

The world is familiar with the usual Southern defense of lynching. Passing by the number, place, and race of the victims, the defense centers on the fourth statement above made; and our public men and our writers have long insisted that this terrible and lawless vengeance is visited upon the defilers of our homes, who should be as ruthlessly destroyed as they have destroyed our domestic purity and peace. This is the regular plea put forth in defense of this brutal practice, warmly maintained by hot-blooded and misinformed people in private and in the public prints. No less a person that a former Judge Advocate-General of Virginia, in a recent issue of the *North American Review,* reiterates these threadbare statements.

He says: "It is unnecessary to shock the sensibilities of the public by calling attention to the repulsive details of those crimes for which lynching, in some form, has been the almost invariable penalty. They have always been, however, of a nature so brutal that no pen can describe and no imagination picture them." "Lynchings in the South are mainly caused by the peculiar nature of the crimes for which lynching is a penalty"; and, more explicitly, "The crime itself, however, is more responsible for mob violence than all other causes combined." "No right thinking man or woman, white or black, ought to have, or can have, any sympathy for such criminals as those who suffer death for the crime described, nor can they believe that any punishment, however cruel or severe, is undeserved." This is a fair type of the usual plea of the Southern advocate. For such a statement as the last quoted to be possible is sufficient evidence of the general sentiment of the section.

But, now, if it were strictly the fact that violent rape is the cause of most of our lynchings; if it were true, moreover, that the man were suddenly and violently slain by the husband, lover, father, brother, of the dishonored one, in quick tempest of wrath and agony unspeakable—while we must still condemn, we might, in sympathy and sorrow, condone the deed of hurried vengeance. *But neither of these things is true.*

It has been repeatedly shown, in the first place, that only a very small proportion (in some years *one tenth*) of Southern lynchings are due to rape, either actual or suspected. Statistics on the subject may be had for the asking; and in their light it seems about time for our apologists to drop this stock and entirely false pleading. "But the writer in the *Review* cites a case where this plea held good." Granted; but this is advocacy: and for every case so cited from five to ten cases can be cited where it not only did not hold good, but was not even pretended by the workers of mob violence. So, in a recent issue of a noted and rabid Southern daily a case of lynching for rape is indicated by large headlines; and just beneath it is a short and insignificant paragraph noting the lynching of *two* Negroes for *suspected* barn-burning. But these latter cases are not mentioned by our advocates; or, if mentioned, are minified by those who feel that our section must be defended at any cost, and so plead.

On the contrary, a frank consideration of all the facts, with no other desire than to find the truth, the whole truth, and nothing but the truth, however contrary to our wishes and humiliating to our section the truth may be, will show that by far the most of our Southern lynchings are carried through in sheer, unqualified, and increasing brutality. In nearly every case, neither the sentiment that prompts them nor the spirit of their execution deserves anything less than the most bitter arraignment. We do, indeed, hear from time to time of an "orderly body of leading citizens" conducting a lynching. But, while the writer knows of certainly one instance where this took place—the accused being, however, a white man known as guilty, and put to death in the most painless possible way with chloroform by those nearest and dearest to his victim—it is fortunately a much rarer occurrence than our newspapers would have us believe. Our lynchings are the work of our lower and lowest classes. What these classes are is hardly comprehensible to one who has not lived among them and dealt with them.

One adult white man in the South in every six or eight can neither read nor write; and if the standard be put above the level of most rudimentary literacy the disproportion rapidly increases. A generation before our Civil War, George Bourne charged the Southern slaveholders with "self-conceit," "marble-hearted insensibility," total lack of "correct views of equity," and "violence in cruelty." Whether applicable, as used by Mr. Bourne, or not, this terrible indictment at once intimates the origin of our present views and treatment of the Negro, and may be applied today, in every term, to the classes that supply our lynchers. Wholly ignorant, absolutely without culture, apparently without even the capacity to appreciate the nicer feelings or higher sense, yet conceited on account of the white skin which they continually dishonor, they make up, when aroused, as wild and brutal a mob as ever disgraced the face of the earth. For them, lynching is not "justice," however rude; it is a wild and diabolic carnival of blood.

No candid man who has seen the average lynching mob, or talked with the average lyncher, can deceive himself for a moment with the idea that this is the expression of a public sentiment righteously indignant over the violation of the law and its impotence or delay. This, too, is a common Southern plea; but it is pure pretense. The lyncher is not, even under ordinary circumstances, over-zealous for the law; and in this case he is not its custodian, but himself its violator. As for the law's delay or inefficiency, the lyncher does not wait to see what the law will do; and yet it is a well-known fact in the South that in the case of a Negro, where violent rape is proven, the punishment of the law is both swift and sure. And in other crimes as well, it is known that the Negro will receive at the hands of the constituted authorities the same, perhaps even a little sharper justice than is meted out to the white man. But as the lyncher sees it, the case stands thus: A Negro has committed or is supposed to have committed a crime. A Negro—and the rest follows. There may be some maudlin talk about the "dreadful crime," about "upholding the majesty of the law," about "teaching the niggers a lesson"; yet the lyncher is but little concerned with the crime, less with the law. As for "teaching the niggers a lesson," that catch phrase of the lynching mob betrays its whole attitude and temper. It would teach the Negro the lesson of abject and eternal servility, would burn into his quivering flesh the consciousness that he has not, and cannot have, the rights of a free citizen or even of a fellow human creature. And so the lyncher seizes his opportunity at once to teach this lesson and to gratify the brute in his own soul, which the thin veneer of his elemental civilization has not been able effectually to conceal.

A recent experience of the writer's may serve to illustrate. A murder had been committed in one of our Southern states. On a night train, returning to the capital of the state, were a marshal and several deputies. Word had gone before that these officers had in charge a Negro, *suspected* of being the murderer; and at four stations in less than forty miles, as many mobs were gathered to mete out summary vengeance to the merely suspected black. Fortunately, the Negro was not on the train. Had he been, his life were not worth the asking; and he would have been most fortunate to find a speedy end on the nearest tree. It cannot be supposed that these mobs were composed of friends and kinsmen of the murdered man. Probably not one quarter of them had ever heard of him previous to the murder, and fewer knew him. They were not orderly bodies of leading citizens, nor of the class in which one would usually find the upholders of the law; but they were coarse, and beastly, and drunk, mad with the terrible blood-lust that wild beasts know, and hunting a human prey.

Take another instance. The burning of Sam Hose took place on a Sabbath day. One of our enterprising railroads ran two special trains to the scene. And two trainloads of men and *boys,* crowding from cowcatcher to the tops of the coaches, were found to go to see the indescribable and sickening torture and writhing of a fellow human being. And souvenirs of such scenes are sought— knee caps, and finger bones, and bloody ears. It is the purest savagery.

The utter shallowness and hypocrisy of this Southern plea that this is a righteous public sentiment, aroused and administering a rude but terrible justice, is patent and undeniable, and can be shown in the clearest light by a single simple proposition. White men commit the same crimes, and worse, against the black man, for which the black man pays this terrible and ungodly penalty.

Can any sane man, white or black, North or South, suppose for a single instant that a Southern community would either permit a black mob to lynch a white man, whether merely suspected or known as guilty of his crime, or that a white mob would lynch one of its own color for any crime against a black? The idea is inconceivable. The color of the victim's skin is the determining factor in most of our lynchings.

And yet, the home of the Negro is as sacred as that of the white man; his right to live as truly God-given. If the Negro can be kicked and cuffed and cursed rightly, so can the white man. If there is no wrong in dishonoring a Negro's home, there is no more wrong in dishonoring the white man's. If the Negro criminal may be burned at the stake with the usual accompaniments of fiendish cruelty, a white man guilty of the same crime deserves, and should suffer, the same penalty. There is nothing in a white skin, *or a black,* to nullify the essential rights of man as man. And yet to the average Southern white man this manifestly just view seems both disloyal and absurd.

It is useless to speak of any solution of the Negro question while the condition of public sentiment above described continues to exist. The Negro's poverty is, in the main, the result of the regular operation of economic laws; his ignorance is the result of several, but, in general, very natural causes; his social position is, aside from general sentiment, the result of a manifest inferiority and antipathy of race; so that any effort satisfactorily to solve his problem on any of these lines, not touching the root of the matter, cannot hope to meet with any large success. The radical difficulty is not with the Negro, but with the white man! So long as the Negro is popularly regarded and dealt with as he is today, his problem will remain unsolved, and any views as to its solution or "passing" under present conditions are optimistic in the extreme. Indeed, it may be fairly said that, as things now are, the educational, financial, or social advancement of the Negro will only serve to render more acute the situation in the South.

It is not necessary, nor desired, that the Negro should be the social equal of the white man. His political privileges may be curtailed, and without injustice or offense, provided the curtailment work impartially among blacks and whites alike. If fifty percent of the Negroes are deprived of the right of suffrage by reason of illiteracy, and the same legislation is fairly permitted to work the disenfranchisement of all whites (fifteen to twenty percent of our voting population) of the same class, no injustice is done, and there is no ground for complaint. His economic and educational condition may be left to the operation of natural and statute laws, fairly administered. For it is certainly most unwise in any case to surround him with artificial conditions, and to create in him artificial ideas, ideals, or desires.

The development of a free people is a process of law—the gradual unfolding and expansion of the inherent potentialities of the race. If they are capable of advancement, they will inevitably advance; if not, they will as inevitably fail and fall out; and no artificial conditions, temporarily created, can permanently affect the operation of this law.

Yet it will not do, on this principle, to say, as is so often said in the South, that the Negro has had his chance and has failed. He is but a generation from servitude and almost complete illiteracy. During that time he has lived under the cloud of his former state, and in the miasmic atmosphere of unfriendliness and repression. That he has made any progress is strange; that he has made the progress that he has is little short of wonderful. For the development of a servile people cannot be measured by the standards of the free. But freedom is not a matter of form and statute only. No people is free whose simple human privileges and possibilities are curtailed or denied by the public sentiment that surrounds them. No people is free that is dominated and terrorized by a more numerous and powerful class. No people is free whose inherent rights to life, liberty, and the pursuit of happiness, how much soever guaranteed by the organic law, are, in practice and in fact, held on sufferance, and constantly at the mercy of a lawless mob.

Freedom does not, indeed, imply social, intellectual, or moral equality; but its very essence is the equality of the fundamental rights of human creatures before God and the law. Such freedom is not a human institution; and no man or men have any right inhering in their birth, color, or traditions, to tamper with or curtail such freedom at their arbitrary pleasure, or in accordance with the dictates of their frenzied passions. Such men are violators of the law, both human and divine.

And here lies the remedy for the condition of things as existing in the South. The white man who wrongs a black and the white mob that lynches a Negro have, by that act and to that extent, become criminals in the eyes of the law, and should be dealt with unsparingly as such. It should no longer be a notable thing, to be chronicled in the news columns and elicit editorial comment, that several white men should be punished for the brutal murder of one inoffensive Negro. It should be the rule. And as for lynching—let all the officers of the law, with all the powers of the law, defend the rights and life of every prisoner. Surely we who can revel in the burning of a fellow human being, and a section some of whose prominent men can soberly defend such a bloody proceeding, ought not to have any over-sensitive scruples at the shedding of a little additional blood, and that too of criminals caught in the very act of crime. So let our marshals have instructions, failure to obey which shall result in criminal prosecution, to protect at any cost the accused who come into their care.

If this seems bloody, is it more bloody than the lyncher's purpose? Or is he any the more a murderer who, in silence and alone, takes the life of a fellow man, than every member of a mob which, without the process of the law, takes a human life? And if the mob calls murder a justification for its course of vengeance, does it not, by its own act and attitude, condemn itself to a like penalty? At any rate, this is the only restraining influence that our lynchers can comprehend, and this, together with the most rigid administration of the law in the case of every wrong done to a Negro, is the only available remedy for conditions as they now exist. Our lower classes must be *made* to realize, by whatever means, that the black man has rights which they are *bound* to respect.

This is the heart of the Southern problem of the Negro. If we call upon the people of the North to give over their mistaken ideas of the equality of the races in superficial and accidental things, we are called upon by the louder voice of simple humanity to give over our much more vicious idea of the inequality of the races in the fundamental rights of human creatures. If we call upon them to lay aside sentiment, we must lay aside cruelty. If they are not to elevate the Negro above his proper sphere, we are not to debase him to the level of the brute. But in mutual understanding, a frank (if sorrowful) recognition of all the facts—of the limitations of the race on the one hand, and of its inalienable rights on the other, with charity and good will between North and South, and of both toward the black man—let us give him fair and favorable conditions, and suffer him to work out, unhampered, his destiny among us.

JOHN SPENCER BASSETT

Heretical views on the racial question emanated from not one but two small Methodist colleges located in the South in the very early years of the twentieth century—from Emory College and the pen of Andrew Sledd in 1902, and from Trinity College in Durham, North Carolina, in 1903. John Spencer Bassett, professor of history at Trinity, was the instigator of the crisis which soon enveloped all Trinity College. Like Sledd, Bassett was of Virginia ancestry, but his family had moved to eastern North Carolina just before the Civil War. Bassett was born there, in Tarboro, in 1867. Graduating from Trinity in 1888 (then located in Randolph County), he taught there briefly before going on to Johns Hopkins University where he received the Ph.D. degree in 1894. He then returned to Trinity (located in Durham since 1892) where he became a leading teacher and scholar.

Reading the famous Bassett essay today, containing the author's admission of his own racial prejudices, it is hard to believe that even in 1903 it could have raised such a howling tempest. Certainly it is one of the mildest essays included in the present volume. That it did create so much excitement was undoubtedly due to a number of factors. First, there was Bassett's declaration that Booker T. Washington was "the greatest man, save General Lee, born in the South in a hundred years." While a strong case could be made for the veracity of the statement, it was a needless provocation to the white South, which completely ignored all the qualifications with which Bassett hedged it about. Second, there was Bassett's just but blunt attack on "political editors" who "stirred up the fires of race antipathy." Josephus Daniels of the Raleigh *News and Observer* rightly interpreted this as an attack on him personally, and as North Carolina's leading editor— especially in anti-Negro attitudes—he set out to "get" the heretic from Trinity College. Finally, there was the determination, by Bassett, Trinity President John Carlisle Kilgo, and the Duke family, to make the issue one of academic freedom. Bassett refused to resign unless the trustees asked for his resignation, and by a vote of eighteen to seven the trustees decided to uphold him.

By refusing to yield to popular demand for the resignation of a faculty member who had challenged the whole climate of race baiting, Trinity College earned for itself newfound recognition and respect. It took the turn which led it to become a great university— Duke—when it might more easily have bowed before the popular clamor. Bassett, too, gained a greater measure of fame and respect than he might otherwise have been expected to attain. In 1906 opportunity beckoned him to Smith College. There, until his accidental death in 1928, he continued to pour forth a stream of writings on American history. Today, among one group and at least in one place in the South, John Spencer Bassett's is not a forgotten voice. To the alumni of Duke University and on the campus at Durham, the story of the "Bassett Affair" is proud history which blends into legend.

Stirring up
The Fires of Race
Antipathy

WHATEVER be his view of the Negro problem, the average American knows that in the last five years there has been a notable increase in the general opposition to the Negro. This development has occurred in both the South and the North. In the South it has manifested itself more strenuously than in the North. We see it there in restrictions on the Negro vote, in the passage of laws for "Jim Crow" cars, in an increasing resort to lynching, and in a general augmentation of that sensitive disposition on the part of Southerners to take fire at the hint of a "Negro outrage." In the North it is seen, but not nearly so plainly as in the South, and it is especially noticeable because in that section it was supposed formerly not to exist at all. It is manifested in occasional acts of violence, as the recent lynching in Delaware, and in a growing opinion which one finds expressed in newspapers and in private conversation with Northern men. This opinion in the North is most strongly held in the large cities and it is noteworthy that in most of the large Northern cities there is a rapid increase of the Negro population.*

The causes of this development are perhaps numerous. But there are three facts which lie at its bottom and which are worthy of special consideration. These are inherent race antipathy, the progress of the Negro himself, and the fact that the Negro problem is, and has been for a long time, a political matter.

Race antipathy is as old as the Negro's residence in America. From the earliest days he has been regarded by the whites as an

*Reprinted from the *South Atlantic Quarterly*, II (October, 1903), 297-305.

inferior man, and a man with whom unrestricted communication on the part of the whites is degrading. Eleven years after the landing of the first Negro in Virginia this idea received a striking illustration in a decision of the highest court in the colony. It was decreed, says the chronicler, "that Hugh Davis be soundly whipped, before an assembly of Negroes and others for abusing himself to the dishonor of God and shame of christians, by defiling his body in lying with a Negro; which fault he is to acknowledge next Sabbath day." In 1726 the Reverend John Blacknall, of North Carolina, was fined fifty pounds for marrying a white man and a mulatto woman. The commingling which we then set our hearts against in regard to things sexual we have also opposed in regard to most other matters of life. There must be no social equality, not eating together, no joining in amusements, and finally no mingling in religious worship. This feeling has not always appeared on the surface. It has frequently been so well covered over by indifference or opportunism, as to be nearly invisible, but if one will but scratch hard enough he will find it beneath this outer covering.

This antipathy is not mutual. It is not the white man against the Negro and the Negro against white man. It is not distasteful to the Negro to eat his dinner or go to churches or to theaters with white men. He is quite willing to have equality. The race feeling is the contempt of the white man for the Negro. It is the reaction of the superior against the touch of the inferior; for the white man has no doubt of his own superiority. It is doubtful if the average Southern white farmer would admit that the highest Negro in America is superior to the Southern hired man who is white.

The development of the Negro since the war has been calculated to intensify this natural race feeling. Singularly enough both his progress and his regression under the regime of freedom have brought down on him the hostility of the whites. His regression might well do this because it has stood for his lapse into a lower state after the removal of the supporting hand of the white man. This lapse has not occurred in all sections of the race—perhaps it has not occurred with a majority of the race—but there can be no denial that some Negroes today are more worthless than any Negroes in slavery. The master was always a restraining hand on the Negro, holding back at both extremes. He kept the slave man from going into the higher fields of intellectual development; he confirmed his lack of high moral purpose; and he weighed down his self-respect and his individuality, all of which were checks on the best Negroes. On the other hand the master was a check on the lowest tendencies of the Negro. He restrained his dissipations; he sought to save him from disease; he tried to make him honest and peaceable; and he was very careful that he should not be an idler. The removal of the masters' authority has produced a marked change on each of these extremes. The upper-class Negro has seized with surprising readiness his new opportunity. No sensible man in the North or in the South who is not blinded by passion will deny that the better Negroes of the country have made a remarkable record since the days of emancipation. In the same way the lower class have also made a rapid progress. Among them idleness and shiftlessness have increased; petty crimes and quarrels have increased; coarse ideas have found greater sway; and viciousness has augmented. These good and these bad habits are the fruits of his freedom.

Neither of these two classes, the upper and the lower, are all the Negroes; and in forgetting this fact some well-intentioned people have fallen into serious error. A man whose mind runs away into baseless optimism is apt to point to Booker T. Washington as a product of the Negro race. Now Washington is a great and good man, a Christian statesman, and take him all in all the greatest man, save General Lee, born in the South in a hundred years; but he is not a typical Negro. He does not even represent the better class of Negroes. He is an exceptional man; and, endowed as he is, it is probable that he would have remained uneducated but for the philanthropic intervention of white men. The race, even the best of them, are so far behind him that we cannot in reason look for his reproduction in the present generation. It is, therefore, too much to hope for a continued appearance of such men in the near future. It is also too much to set his development up as a standard for his race. To expect it is to insure disappointment.

In the same way some people who are pessimistic in regard to the Negro base their opinions on their observations of the Negro of the lowest class. Said a gentleman to me recently: "The Negro race will die out within a century." His reason was this: a few years ago there were sixteen Negroes in the jail of his county, and the county physician had told him that fifteen of them had venereal diseases. From this he argued that the physical constitution of the race was imperiled. Manifestly, it is illogical to measure either the health, morals, or other quality of the Negro by the similar quality of the most depraved. It is true that there is in the race a large lowest class—and a small upper class. And it is true that this lowest class gives the race a certain discouraging tendency. But there is also a strong, and perhaps an increasing, upper class which is ever fighting back its own weakness and shaking off its own shackles.

In this connection I cannot refrain from speaking of a certain false notion in regard to the Negro which has caused much error in the opinions of men North and South. I refer to the notion that the ante-bellum Negro was a benign old man or a gracious old "mammy," a guardian of the family honor. The falseness of this notion is due partly to the imagination of certain novelists and partly to the emotional memories of most Southern women and some Southern men. As to the latter it is pardonable failing. A woman may well remember her old "mammy" and have no recollection of hare-lipped Peter who ran away with a long scar across his forehead, as the advertisements put it. But men who undertake to describe the life of the old South ought to know what it was before they talk about it. Mr. Thomas Nelson Page's castles in Virginia are also castles in the air. The typical ante-bellum Negro was the field hand. When we compare the old and the new Negro we ought to place the new man by the side of that individual. And if we do not remember what kind of a man the field hand of slavery was—for our novelists have not remembered much about him—we may inform ourselves in the instructive pages of Olmsted, or in Fanny Kemble's interesting *Journal*. Nine-tenths of the Negroes now in America are descended from this part of the old slave population.

It is important for us to note that the progress of the Negro has brought him opposition as well as his regression. Of this the white men who oppose him may not be conscious. They may even fancy that they are the best of friends to the Negro. But the advance of the Negro in education and in economic conditions brings him ever into new conflicts with the white man. This is true because his advance means a greater degree of comfort—a greater disposition to desire the means of higher life. As long as he was merely a laborer it was not hard to draw the line which divided him from other people. It was at that time not hard for him to be content with inferior hotels, or with accommodations in the kitchens of better hotels. In these days he is becoming too intelligent and too refined to be content with these things. He demands a better place. Formerly, it did not hurt his pride to ride in a "Jim Crow" car, for he had little or no pride of that kind. Now he considers this law a badge of inferiority, a mark of intolerance which he will some day seek to wipe out.

With most Americans there is a very definite notion that the Negro has his "place." In their minds this notation is a caste feeling. It is an inherent feeling; and it is not difficult to find facts in the Negro's life which seem to give it the support of expediency. To make him know his "place" and to make him keep his "place" sum up the philosophy of many people in reference to this intricate and perplexing problem. But we ought to remember that such an idea is neither scientific nor charitable. The "place" of every man in our American life is such a one as his virtues and his capacities may enable him to take. Not even a black skin and a flat nose can justify caste in this country.

The most aggravating cause, however, of the present antipathy between the races is the fact that the Negro question is in politics. It has been in politics since the day when the Negro became the chief factor in American labor. It was so in Georgia in the days of the benevolent Oglethorpe, when the chief political desire of the people was the admission of Negro slaves. It appeared in the great constitutional convention of 1787, when certain Southern states spoke darkly of the future in case they should not be allowed to import slaves. It was a political question in the two angry decades which preceded the Civil War, when abolition fires burned fiercely on the one side and pro-slavery fires on the other. It was still in politics in 1860 and 1861, when eleven states seceded from the Union rather than run the risk of having the "black Republicans" abolish slavery. It was still a political question in the days of constitutional amendment and in the reactionary days of 1875. It has become a political question in another form within the last ten years. Whatever concerns our secular life we undertake to regulate by political action; and it is not strange that we have so often brought law to bear on this question.

But the Negro question has gone into politics recently in a party, rather than in a truly political sense. It has been seized upon by party leaders as a means of winning votes. This has been particularly true in the South. Always since 1875 the Southern Democratic campaigners have used the Negro issue with good effect. A certain brilliant party leader, who now holds a large share of public attention, used in the early days of his career to make his best appeal to the gaping audiences at the country crossroads by asking all the men who wanted to vote the white man's ticket to pass to one side of the road and all who would vote the black man's ticket to stay where they were. When the crowd began to move across the road it was hard for a white man to stand in his tracks. That was the worst manifestation of this form of the issue twenty years ago.

Ten years ago the South was in the embrace of the Populist movement, designed by its leaders to organize the mass of farmers into a political association. This movement, if successful, would have broken up the Democratic party. It was strong enough to make itself dreaded by the party. To fight it down the leaders of the old party were led to seek a strong issue. The Negro issue was selected. It lent itself to the exigency because the Populists, wherever they triumphed, had been in alliance with the Republicans and had brought a few Negroes into office. These Negroes were usually quietly disposed, but they were frequently unfit for office; and the very fact that they were Negroes made it impossible for them to execute their offices on white men. They were also sometimes unduly elated over their success, being merely ignorant Negroes. The result was various conflicts. This gave an opportunity to cry "Negro domination." Raising the cry by the one side produced irritation on the other side, and the very denunciation of Negroes for "outrages" produced a continuation of the "outrages." From that time to this the Negro issue in the South has taken on a new phase.

In order to insure its ascendancy the old party passed the suffrage amendments. It promised the people that if they would by this means eliminate the Negro vote the old condition of a solid white party would disappear and that we should have no more cheating of Negroes out of their votes. The success of these campaigns convinced the leaders that the issue was a popular one. Having won a complete success they are loath, in spite of their promise, to give up the means by which they succeeded. It is now good party tactics to keep the Negro question before the people. Booker T. Washington's dinner at the White House was seized on for this purpose. The watchful party leaders saw in it an opportunity to make capital with the mass of the people. Not long after this there occurred in Washington what has been known since that time as the "biracial reception." This, too, at once suggested itself as a popular means of appealing to the people.

So successful were these two attempts that some political editors have learned to look for similar occasions. At present very inconsiderable affairs are made to do service in the same way. An illustration of how this works is seen in the following incident: In the

month of August, 1903, Booker T. Washington and a party of
prominent Negroes, most of them Northern men, were going North
after the adjournment of a Negro businessmen's conference in
Knoxville, Tennessee. He telegraphed to the proprietors of a certain dinner-house on the railroad to know if, on the arrival of the
train, he and his party could be given breakfast. The reply was
favorable. When the train arrived the regular boarders had been
served. The party of Negroes, which numbered thirty-eight, were
given seats in the regular dining room. The proprietors understood
that there were no white people on the train who desired breakfast, but a few presented themselves and tables were improvised
for them in other rooms. The Negroes, according to the evidence,
bore themselves quietly and unobtrusively. There was no attempt
to mix the races. It was not alleged that the accommodations of the
one were not as good as those of the other. This incident became
in the hands of politicians a flagrant "outrage." A certain emotional and "yellow" newspaper was conspicuous in its lurid de-
scriptions. Black men, it said, were placed before white men.
Formerly a white man ate at the first table and sent the Negro's
dinner out to the kitchen. Now the Negro took the principal seat
and the whites took what they could get. It gave a long and hysterical description of this very small affair and ended with the observation that the whole thing was due to the fact that President Roosevelt once had Professor Washington to dine with him. Following
the lead of this prominent newspaper a hundred smaller sheets
took up the matter in the same vein; and the dinner-house affair
now became very much of a sensation. Day after day for more
than a fortnight it continually reappeared in the state press, and
the echoes of it are still heard.

The effect of such agitation on the people is decided. It un-
questionably tends to make votes. The removal of the Negro from
the voting population has destroyed the oldest and best political
capital of the party; and its place is being supplied by these sensa-
tional appeals to the race feeling of the white man. But the affair
has a more serious side. This political agitation is awaking a

demon in the South. There is today more hatred of whites for blacks and of blacks for whites than ever before. Each race seems to be caught in a torrent of passion, which, I fear, is leading the country to an end which I dare not name.

Up in the North a little Southern gentleman with a glib tongue has been going about recently advocating the formation of a black republic in the Philippines to which all the Negroes shall be sent. A man who can solve the Negro problem in no better way than to advocate deportation has but little capacity to solve problems. Worthy old Hinton Rowan Helper, who still lives to hear the first threatening notes of a new *Impending Crisis,* has a more feasible solution, viz: "to fossilize them beneath the American sod." But neither solution will work. The only solution reserved for us is the adoption of these children of Africa into our American life. In spite of our race feeling, of which the writer has his share, they will win equality at some time. We cannot remove them, we cannot kill them, we cannot prevent them from advancing in civilization. They are now very weak; some day they will be stronger. They are now ignorant and passion-wrought; some day they will be wiser and more self-restrained. I do not know just what form the conflict will take. It may be merely a political conflict; it may be more than that. I am persuaded that it is in many respects the old conflict between Roman plebs and Roman patricians over again. It ought to be shorter than that struggle and the issue ought to be more fortunate than the issue of the Roman conflict; for American life is richer and better than Roman life.

Someday the white man will beat the Negro out of his cowardice, and then "red shirts" will exist no more. Someday the Negro will be a great industrial factor in the community; someday he will be united under strong leaders of his own. In that time his struggle will not be so unequal as now. In that time, let us hope, he will have brave and Christian leaders.

The writer has no solution for the Negro problem. He does not think that it can be solved by writing magazine articles or by making speeches. It is the manifestation of a great social force, which will run its course in spite of our laying on of hands. The best we can do is to understand this force as fully as possible, and probably to check in a measure some of its most erratic impulses. We are now just entering the stage of conflict; and this is because the Negro is now beginning to be strong enough to make opposition. The conflict will be fiercer in the future than in the present. Lynchings and "outrages" will, perhaps, become more frequent than they are now. As long as one race contends for the absolute inferiority of the other the struggle will go on with increasing intensity. But if someday the spirit of conciliation shall come into the hearts of the superior race the struggle will become less strenuous. The duty of brave and wise men is to seek to infuse the spirit of conciliation into these white leaders of white men. Shall they also be beasts, like the dull-faced black men who stand over against them? Is the white man not superior to the black man— superior in mind, superior in opportunity, superior in obligation to do acts of charity?

QUINCY EWING

The Reverend Quincy Ewing was the center of a storm of contention most of his life. Brilliant, handsome, and individualistic, he chafed under the hand of episcopal authority and challenged the status quo from every quarter. Had he been less disputatious, he undoubtedly would have advanced much further in the hierarchy of the Episcopal church, but then we probably would have had little reason to remember him as the fearless foe of all forms of injustice, which he was.

Born near Thibodaux, Louisiana, in 1877, and educated at Sewanee, the University of the South, Ewing spent twenty-three years of his clerical career at Christ Church, Napoleonville, Louisiana, less than a dozen miles from where he was born. Before he returned to Napoleonville in 1906—to the church which had been built by his grandfather—he was the first dean of Christ Church Cathedral, New Orleans, and held charges in Ohio, Mississippi, and Alabama. All of these years were stormy ones, particularly those in Mississippi, where he publicly and in print denounced the crime of lynching and fought the state's leading racist, James K. Vardaman. After fifteen years of ecclesiastical, social, and racial battles, Ewing returned to the relative quiet of Napoleonville and the land of his forebears. For the next twenty years he served the Christ Church congregation and wrote dozens of articles, essays, and letters to editors on such subjects as theology, the Negro, woman suffrage, and other controversial topics.

Napoleonville in 1909 was a tiny (population 1,201 in 1910), untypical Southern town, located in Assumption Parish, sixty miles west of New Orleans. More than ninety percent of the population were Roman Catholics of French descent, with a very low literacy level. The white Anglo-Saxon Protestants who made up the remainder of the population were the real "power structure" of the town, and generally they were communicants of Ewing's Christ Church. In such a community the appearance in the *Atlantic Monthly* of a liberal essay on the race problem and written by the local Episcopal minister created scarcely a ripple. The overwhelming majority of the town doubtless never heard of it, while Ewing's parishioners, though they might disagree with his views, had learned to live with and even ignore them. After all, he was from a good and old local family; he was related by blood or marriage to many of his parishioners; and he had married a descendant of the Carters of Shirley plantation.

In his essay "The Heart of the Race Problem" Ewing charged, that to the white South the Negro was not a problem because of his blackness, his crime rate, his low morals, and his inferior state of development, but rather because the whites were determined to keep him from ever standing on "common human ground." Or, stated differently, the race problem was "the problem [of] how to keep the Negro in focus" with the traditional viewpoint. Even in the Episcopal Church, traditionally more liberal on social issues, there was little room for a Southern minister of such views in the early years of the twentieth century. But not until 1929 did he leave Napoleonville, to accept the charge of St. James Church, Lindsay, California. It was from there that he retired in 1935 to Ocean Springs, Mississippi. He died in New Orleans in 1939 and was buried in the family lot at Thibodaux.

The Heart
of the Race Problem

D URING the past decade, newspaper and magazine articles
galore, and not a few books, have been written on what is
called the "Race Problem," the problem caused by the presence
in this country of some ten millions of black and variously-shaded
colored people known as Negroes. But, strange as it may sound,
the writer has no hesitation in saying that at this date there appears
to be no clear conception anywhere, on the part of most people, as
to just what the essential problem is which confronts the white
inhabitants of the country because they have for fellow-citizens
(nominally) ten million Negroes. Ask the average man, ask even
the average editor or professor anywhere, what the race problem
is, the heart of it; why, in this land with its millions of foreigners
of all nationalities, *the* race problem of problems should be caused
by ten million Negroes, not foreigners but native to the soil
through several generations; and in all probability you will get
some such answer as this:*

"The Negroes, as a rule, are very ignorant, are very lazy, are
very brutal, are very criminal. But a little way removed from
savagery, they are incapable of adopting the white man's moral
code, of assimilating the white man's moral sentiments, of striv-
ing toward the white man's moral ideals. They are creatures of
brutal, untamed instincts, and uncontrolled feral passions, which
give frequent expression of themselves in crimes of horrible
ferocity. They are, in brief, an uncivilized, semi-savage people,
living in a civilization to which they are unequal, partaking to a

*Reprinted from *Atlantic Monthly,* CIII (March, 1909), 389–97.

limited degree of its benefits, performing in no degree its duties. Because they are spatially in a civilization to which they are morally and intellectually repugnant, they cannot but be as a foreign irritant to the body social. The problem is, how shall the body social adjust itself, daily, hourly, to this irritant; how feel at ease and safe in spite of it? How shall the white inhabitants of the land, with their centuries of inherited superiority, conserve their civilization and carry it forward to a yet higher plane, hampered by ten million black inhabitants of the same land with their centuries of inherited inferiority?"

To the foregoing answer, this might now and again be added, or advanced independently in reply to our question: "Personal aversion on the part of the white person for the Negro; personal aversion accounted for by nothing the individual Negro is, or is not, intellectually and morally; accounted for by the fact, simply, that he is a Negro, that he has a black or colored skin, that he is different, of another kind."

Now, certainly, there are very few average men or philosophers, to whom the answer given to our question would not seem to state, or at any rate fairly indicate, the race problem in its essence. But, however few they be, I do not hesitate to align myself with them as one who does not believe that the essential race problem as it exists in the South (whatever it be in the North) is stated, or even fairly indicated, in the foregoing answer. In Northern and Western communities, where he is outnumbered by many thousands of white people, the Negro may be accounted a problem, because he is lazy, or ignorant, or brutal, or criminal, or all these things together; or because he is black and different. But in Southern communities, where the Negro is not outnumbered by many thousands of white people, the race problem, essentially, and in its most acute form, is something distinct from his laziness or ignorance, or brutality, or criminality, or all-round intellectual and moral inferiority to the white man. That problem as the South knows and deals with it would exist, as certainly as it does to-day, if there were no shadow of excuse for the conviction that the

Negro is more lazy, or more ignorant, or more criminal, or more brutal, or more anything else he ought not to be, or less anything else he ought to be, than other men. In other words, let it be supposed that the average Negro is as a matter of fact the equal, morally and intellectually, of the average white man of the same class, and the race problem declines to vanish, declines to budge. We shall see why, presently. The statements just made demand immediate justification. For they are doutbless surprising to a degree, and to some readers may prove startling.

I proceed to justify them as briefly as possible, asking the reader to bear in mind that very much more might be said along this line than I allow myself space to say.

That the Negro is not a problem because he is lazy, because he declines to work, is evidenced by the patent fact that in virtually every Southern community he is sought as a laborer in fields, mills, mines, and that in very many Southern communities the vexing problem for employers is not too many, but too few Negroes. In certain agricultural sections, notably in the Louisiana sugar district, quite a number of Italians ("Dagoes") are employed. The reason is not dissatisfaction with Negro labor, but simply that there is not enough of it to meet the requirements of the large plantations. There is, perhaps, not one of these plantations on which any able-bodied Negro could not get employment for the asking; and as a rule, the Negroes are given, not the work which demands the lowest, but that which demands the highest, efficiency; they are the ploughmen, the teamsters, the foremen. If any one doubts that Negroes are wanted as laborers in Southern communities, very much wanted, let him go to any such community and attempt to inveigle a few dozen of the laziest away. He will be likely to take his life in his hands, after the usual warning is disregarded!

The small politician's trump card, played early and late, and in all seasons, that the Negro is a black shadow over the Southland because of his excessive criminality, serves well the politician's purpose—it wins his game; but only because the game is played and won on a board where fictions, not facts, are dominant.

Nothing is easier than to offer so-called proofs of the contention that the Negro's tendency to crime is something peculiar to his race; there are the jail and penitentiary and gallows statistics, for instance. But surely it should not be difficult for these so-called proofs to present themselves in their true light to any one who takes the trouble to consider two weighty and conspicuous facts: this, first, that the Negroes occupy everywhere in this country the lowest social and industrial plane, the plane which everywhere else supplies the jail, the penitentiary, the gallows, with the greatest number of their victims; and secondly this, that in the section of the country where these penal statistics are gathered, all the machinery of justice is in the hands of white men.

No Negro is a sheriff, or judge, or justice of the peace, or grand or petit juryman, or member of a pardoning board. Charged with crime, again and again, the black man must go to jail; he is unable to give bond; he is defended, not by the ablest, but by the poorest lawyers, often by an unwilling appointee of the court; he lacks the benefit of that personal appeal to judge and jury, so often enjoyed by other defendants, which would make them *want* to believe him innocent until proven guilty; he faces, on the contrary, a judge and jury who hold him in some measure of contempt as a man, regardless of his guilt or innocence. He is without means, except occasionally, to fight his case through appeals to higher courts, and errors sleep in many a record that on review would upset the verdict. In the light of such considerations, it would seem impossible that criminal statistics should not bear hard upon the Negro race, even supposing it to be a fact that that race of all races in the world is the *least* criminal.

Let it be admitted without question that in most southern communities the crimes and misdemeanors of the Negroes exceed those committed by an equal number of white people, and we have admitted nothing that at all explains or accounts for the race problem. For is it not equally true that in every other community the doers of society's rough work, the recipients of its meagrest rewards, are chargeable, relatively, with the greatest number of crimes and misdemeanors? Is it not true, as well in Massachusetts and Connecticut as in Louisiana and Mississippi, that the vast majority of those occupying prison cells are members of the social lowest class; that the vast majority condemned, after trial, to hard labor with their hands were accustomed to such labor before their judicial condemnation? Nothing is more preposterous than the idea that the race problem means more Negroes hanged, more Negroes imprisoned, more Negroes in mines and chain gangs, than white people! If the Negro did not furnish the great bulk of the grist for the grinding of our penal machinery in the Southern states, he would constitute the racial miracle of this and all ages!

My own conviction is, and I speak with the experience of forty years' residence in Southern states, that the Negro is not more given to crimes and misdemeanors than the laboring population of any other section of the country. But be this as it may, it is abundantly certain that no race of people anywhere are more easily controlled than the Negroes by the guardians of law and order; and there are none anywhere so easily punished for disobedience to the statutes and mandates of their economic superiors. Courts and juries may be sometimes subject to just criticism for undue leniency toward white defendants; but that courts and juries are ever subject to just criticism for undue leniency in dealing with black defendants is the sheerest nonsense.

The frequent charge that the Negro's worst crimes partake of a brutality that is peculiarly racial, is not supported by facts. I need not enlarge upon this statement further than to say that the Negro's worst crimes, with all their shocking accompaniments, are, not seldom, but often, duplicated by white men. Let any one who doubts the statement observe for one week the criminal statistics of any cosmopolitan newspaper, and he will have his doubt removed.

Assuredly we do not hit upon the essence of the race problem in the Negro's propensity to crime!

Do we hit upon it in his ignorance, in the fact that an immense number of the black people are illiterate, not knowing the first from the last letter of the alphabet? Hardly. For, almost to a man, the people who most parade and most rail at the race problem in private conversation, on the political platform, and in the pages of newspapers, books, and periodicals, are disposed rather to lament, than to assist, the passing of the Negro's ignorance. Ex-governor Vardaman, of Mississippi, used the following language in a message to the legislature of that state, January, 1906:

> The startling facts revealed by the census show that those [Negroes] who can read and write are more criminal than the illiterate, which is true of no other element of our population. . . . The state for many years, at great expense to the tax-payers, has maintained a system of Negro education which has produced disappointing results, and I am opposed to the perpetuation of this system. My own idea is, that the character of education for the Negro ought to be changed. If, after forty years of earnest effort, and the expenditure of fabulous sums to educate his head, we have only succeeded in making a criminal of him and impairing his usefulness and efficiency as a laborer, wisdom would suggest that we make another experiment and see if we cannot improve him by educating his hand and his heart. . . . Slavery is the only process by which he has ever been partially civilized. God Almighty created the Negro for a menial, he is essentially a servant.

This is the reply of an ex-governor of one of our blackest states to those who contend that the Negro is a problem, a "burden carried by the white people of the South," because of his ignorance and consequent inefficiency; and that the lightening of the burden depends upon more money spent, more earnest efforts made, for the schooling of the black people. According to this ex-governor, and there are thousands who agree with him in and out of Mississippi, the race problem is heightened, rather than mitigated, by all attempts to increase the Negro's intellectual efficiency. The more ignorant he is, the less burdensome he is to the white man, provided his heart be good, and his hands skillful enough to do the service of a menial. Nothing but slavery ever partially civilized him, nothing but slavery continued in some form can civilize him further!

If we listen vainly for the heart-throb of the race problem in the Negro's laziness, and criminality, and brutality, and ignorance, and inefficiency, do we detect it with clearness and certainty in the personal aversion felt by the white people for the black people, aversion which the white people can no more help feeling than the black people can help exciting? Is this the real trouble, the real burden, the real tragedy and sorrow of our white population in those sections of the country where the Negroes are many—that they are compelled to dwell face to face, day by day, with an inferior, degraded population, repulsive to their finer sensibilities, obnoxious to them in countless ways inexplicable? Facts are far from furnishing an affirmative answer. However pronounced may be the feeling of personal aversion toward the Negroes in Northern communities, where they are few, or known at long range, or casually, there is no such thing in Southern communities as personal aversion for the Negro pronounced enough to be responsible for anything resembling a problem. How could there be in the South, where from infancy we have all been as familiar with black faces as with white; where many of us fell asleep in the laps of black mammies, and had for playmates Ephrom, Izik, Zeke, black mammy's grandchildren; where most of us have had our meals prepared by black cooks, and been waited on by black house servants and diningroom servants, and ridden in carriages and buggies with black hostlers? We are so used to the black people in the South, their mere personal presence is so far from being responsible for our race problem, that the South would not seem southern without them, as it would not without its crape myrtles, and liveoaks, and magnolias, its cotton and its sugar cane!

It is very easy to go astray in regard to the matter of personal aversion toward the members of alien races, to magnify greatly the reality and importance of it. What seems race aversion is frequently something else, namely, revulsion aroused by the presence of the strange, the unusual, the uncanny, the not-understood. Such revulsion is aroused, not only by the members of alien races, alien and unfamiliar, but as certainly by strange animals of not more terrify-

ing appearance than the well-loved cow and horse; and it would
be aroused as really and as painfully, doubtless, by the sudden
proximity of one of Milton's archangels. It was not necessarily
race aversion which made Emerson, and may have made many
another Concord philosopher, uncomfortable in the presence of a
Negro, any more than it is race aversion which makes the Fifth
Avenue boy run from the gentle farmyard cow; any more than it
is race aversion which would make me uncomfortable in the presence of Li Hung Chang. The Negro, simply, it may be, was a
mystery to Emerson, as the farmyard cow is a mystery to the Fifth
Avenue boy, as the Chinaman is a mystery to me.

The Negro is *not* a mystery to people whom he has nursed
and waited on, whose language he has spoken, whose ways, good
and bad, he has copied for generations; and his personal presence
does not render them uncomfortable not, at any rate, uncomfortable enough to beget the sense of a burden or a problem.

It may be very difficult for Northern readers, to whom the
Negro is in reality a stranger, a foreigner, to appreciate fully the
force of what has just been said; but appreciated by them it must
be, or they can never hope to realize the innermost meaning of
the race problem in the South.

So much for what the race problem is not. Let me without
further delay state what it is. The foundation of it, true or false, is
the white man's conviction, that the Negro as a race, and as an
individual, is his inferior: not human in the sense that he is human,
not entitled to the exercise of human rights in the sense that he is
entitled to the exercise of them. The problem itself, the essence of
it, the heart of it, is the white man's determination to make good
this conviction, coupled with constant anxiety lest, by some means,
he should fail to make it good. The race problem, in other words,
is *not* that the Negro is what he is in relation to the white man,
the white man's inferior; but this, rather: How to keep him what
he is in relation to the white man; how to prevent his ever achiev-
ing or becoming that which would justify the belief on his part,
or on the part of other people, that he and the white man stand
on common human ground.

That such is the heart of the problem should be made evident by this general consideration alone: namely, that everywhere in the South friction between the races is entirely absent so long as the Negro justifies the white man's opinion of him as an inferior; is grateful for privileges and lays no claim to *rights.* Let him seem content to be as the South insists he shall be, and not only is he not harshly treated, not abused, and never boycotted, but he is shown much kindness and generosity, and employment awaits him for the asking. Trouble brews when he begins to manifest those qualities, to reveal those tastes, to give vent to those ambitions, which are supposed to be characteristic exclusively of the higher human type, and which, unless restrained, would result in confounding the lower with the higher. The expression "Good Nigger" means everywhere in the South a real Negro, from the Southern standpoint, one who in no respect gets out of focus with that standpoint; the expression "Bad Nigger" means universally one who in some respect, not necessarily criminal, does get out of focus with it. So, stated differently, the race problem is the problem how to keep the Negro in focus with the traditional standpoint.

But we are very far from needing to rely upon any general consideration in support of the proposition advanced above. It is supported by evidences on every hand, waiting only the eye of recognition. Scarcely a day passes but something is said or done with this end in view, to emphasize, lest they forget, the conviction for both white man and Negro that the latter is and must remain an inferior. Let me instance a few such evidences.

Consider, first, the "Jim Crow" legislation in the manner of its enforcement. Such legislation is supposed to have for its object the separation of the races in trains, streetcars, etc., to save the white people from occasional contact with drunken, rowdy, ill-smelling Negroes, and to prevent personal encounters between the whites and blacks. How is this object attained in the street cars of Southern cities? Members of the different races occupy the same cars, separated only by absurdly inadequate little open-mesh wire screens, so tiny and light that a conductor can move them from one seat to another with the strength of his little finger. Needless to add, these screens would serve to obscure neither sound, sight, nor smell of drunken rowdies who sat behind them! In summer cars black and white passengers may be separated not even by a make-believe screen; they are simply required, respectively, to occupy certain seats in the front or the back end of the cars.

In Birmingham, Alabama, the front seats are assigned to Negroes in all closed cars, and the back seats in all open ones. Why the front seats in the one case, and the back seats in the other, it is not easy to understand in the light of the letter and alleged spirit of the Jim Crow law! The underlying purpose of the law is clearly not the separation of the races in space; for public sentiment does not insist upon its fulfillment to that end. The underlying purpose of it would seem to be the separation of the races in status. The doctrine of inequality would be attacked if white and black passengers rode in public conveyances on equal terms; therefore the Negro who rides in a public conveyance must do so, not as of undoubted right, but as with the white man's permission, subject to the white man's regulation. *"This place you may occupy, that other you may not, because I am I and you are you, lest to you or me it should be obscured that I am I and you are you."* Such is the real spirit of the Jim Crow laws.

Why is it that in every Southern city no Negro is allowed to witness a dramatic performance, or a baseball game, from a first-class seat? In every large city, there are hundreds of Negroes who would gladly pay for first-class seats at the theatre and the baseball game, were they permitted to. It can hardly be that permission is withheld because theatres and baseball games are so well attended by half the population that first-class seats could not be furnished for the other half. As a matter of fact, theatre auditoriums and baseball grandstands are seldom crowded; the rule is, not all first-class seats occupied, but many vacant. Surely as simple as moving from seat to seat a makeshift screen in a streetcar, would it be to set apart a certain number of seats in the dress-circle of every theatre, and in the grandstand of every baseball park, for Negro patrons. The reason why this is not done is perfectly obvious: it would be intolerable to the average Southern man or woman to sit through the hours of a theatrical performance or a baseball game on terms of equal accommodation with Negroes, even with a screen between. Negroes would look out of place, out of status, in the dress circle or the grandstand; their place, signifying their status, is the peanut gallery, or the bleachers. There, neither they nor others will be tempted to forget that as things are they must continue.

How shall we account for the "intense feeling" (to quote the language of the mayor of New Orleans) occasioned in that city one day, last July, when it was flashed over the wires that the first prize in the National Spelling Contest had been won by a Negro girl, in competition with white children from New Orleans and other Southern cities? The indignation of at least one of the leading New Orleans papers verged upon hysterics; the editor's rhetoric visited upon some foulest crime could hardly have been more inflamed than in denunciation of the fact that, on the far-away shore of Lake Erie, New Orleans white children had competed at a spelling bee with a Negro girl. The superintendent of the New Orleans schools was roundly denounced in many quarters for permitting his wards to compete with a Negro; and there were broad hints in "Letters from the People" to the papers that his resignation was in order.

Certainly in the days following the National Spelling Contest the race problem was in evidence, if it ever was, in New Orleans and the South! Did it show itself, then, as the problem of Negro crime, or brutality, or laziness? Assuredly not! Of the Negro's personal repulsiveness? By no means! There was no evidence of Negro criminality, or brutality, or laziness in the Negro child's victory; and every day in the South, in their games and otherwise, hundreds of white children of the best families are in closer personal contact with little Negroes than were the white children who took part in the Cleveland spelling bee. The "intense feeling" can be explained on one ground only: the Negro girl's victory was an affront to the tradition of the Negro's inferiority; it suggested—

perhaps indicated—that, given equal opportunities, all Negroes are not necessarily the intellectual inferiors of all white people. What other explanation is rationally conceivable? If the race problem means in the South to its white inhabitants the burden and tragedy of having to dwell face to face with an intellectually and morally backward people, why should not the Negro girl's triumph have occasioned intense feeling of pleasure, rather than displeasure, by its suggestion that her race is not intellectually hopeless?

Consider further that, while no Negro, no matter what his occupation, or personal refinement, or intellectual culture, or moral character, is allowed to travel in a Pullman car between state lines, or to enter as a guest a hotel patronized by white people, the blackest of Negro nurses and valets are given food and shelter in all first-class hotels, and occasion neither disgust nor surprise in the Pullman cars. Here again the heart of the race problem is laid bare. The black nurse with a white baby in her arms, the black valet looking after the comfort of a white invalid, have the label of their inferiority conspicuously upon them; they understand themselves, and everybody understands them, to be servants, enjoying certain privileges for the sake of the person served. Almost anything, the Negro may do in the South, and anywhere he may go, provided the manner of his doing and his going is that of an inferior. Such is the premium put upon his inferiority; such his inducement to maintain it.

The point here insisted on may be made clearer, if already it is not clear enough, by this consideration, that the man who would lose social caste for dining with an Irish streetsweeper might be congratulated for dining with an Irish educator; but President Roosevelt would scarcely have given greater offense by entertaining a Negro laborer at the White House than he gave by inviting to lunch there the Principal of Tuskegee Institute. The race problem being what it is, the status of any Negro is logically the status of every other. There are recognizable degrees of inferiority among Negroes themselves; some are vastly superior to others. But there is only one degree of inferiority separating the Negro from the white person, attached to all Negroes alike. The logic of the situation requires that to be any sort of black man is to be inferior to any sort of white man; and from this logic there is no departure in the South.

Inconsistent, perhaps, with what has been said may seem the defeat in the Louisiana Legislature (1908) of the antimiscegenation bill, a measure designed to prohibit sexual cohabitation between white persons and Negroes; to be specific, between white men and Negro women. But there was no inconsistency whatever in the defeat of that bill. In all times and places, the status of that portion of the female population, Lecky's martyred "priestesses of humanity," whose existence men have demanded for the gratification of unlawful passion, has been that of social outcasts. They have no rights that they can insist upon; they are simply privileged to exist by society's permission, and may be any moment legislated out of their vocation. Hence the defeat of an antimiscegenation measure by Southern legislators cannot be construed as a failure on their part to live up to their conviction of race superiority. It must be construed, rather, as legislative unwillingness to restrict the white man's liberty; to dictate by statute the kind of social outcast which he may use as a mere means to the gratification of his passion. To concede to Negro women the status of a degraded and proscribed class, is not in any sense to overlook or obscure their racial inferiority, but on the contrary, it may be, to emphasize it. Precisely the same principle, in a word, compasses the defeat of an anti-miscegenation bill which would compass the defeat of a measure to prohibit Negro servants from occupying seats in Pullman cars.

At the risk of reiteration, I must in concluding this article take sharp issue with the view of a recent very able writer, who asks the question, "What, essentially, is the Race Problem?" and answers it thus: "The race problem is the problem of living with human beings who are not like us, whether they are in our estimation our 'superiors' or inferiors, whether they have kinky hair or pigtails, whether they are slant eyed, hook nosed, or thick lipped.

In its essence, it is the same problem magnified, which besets every neighborhood, even every family."

I have contended so far, and I here repeat, that the race problem is essentially *not* what this writer declares it to be. It is emphatically not, in the South, "the problem of living with human beings who are not like us, whether they are in our estimation our superiors or inferiors." It may be, it probably is, that in the North, where the Negro is largely a stranger, a foreigner, very much to the same degree that the Chinese are strangers and foreigners in the South; and where, consequently, the Negro's personal repulsiveness is a much more significant force than it is in the South. Assuredly there would be no race problem anywhere, were there no contact with others unlike ourselves! The unlikeness of the unlike is everywhere its indispensable foundation. But we get nowhither unless we carefully distinguish between the foundation of the problem and the problem itself. There is nothing in the unlikeness of the unlike that is necessarily problematical; it may be simply accepted and dealt with as a fact, like any other fact. The problem arises only when the people of one race are minded to adopt and act upon some policy more or less oppressive or repressive in dealing with the people of another race. In the absence of some such policy, there has never been a race problem since the world began. It is the existence of such a policy become traditional, and supported by immovable conviction, which constitutes the race problem of the Southern states.

There was an immensely tragic race problem distressing the South fifty years ago; but who will suggest that it was the problem of "living with human beings who are not like us?" The problem then was, clearly, how to make good a certain conviction concerning the unlike, how to maintain a certain policy in dealing with them. What else is it today? The problem, how to maintain the institution of chattel slavery, ceased to be at Appomattox; the problem, how to maintain the social, industrial, and civic inferiority of the descendants of chattel slaves, succeeded it, and is the race problem of the South at the present time. There is no other.

Whether the policy adopted by the white South, and supported, as I have said, by immovable conviction, is expedient or inexpedient, wise or unwise, righteous or unrighteous, these are questions which I have not sought to answer one way or another in this article. Perhaps they cannot be answered at all in our time. Certain is it, that their only real and satisfactory answer will be many years ahead of the present generation.

In the meantime, nothing could be more unwarranted than to suppose that the race problem of one section of this country is peculiar to that section, because its white inhabitants are themselves in some sense peculiar; because they are peculiarly prejudiced, because they are peculiarly behind the hour which the high clock of civilization has struck. Remove the white inhabitants of the South, give their place to the white people of any other section of the United States, and, beyond a peradventure, the Southern race problem, as I have defined it, would continue to be—revealed, perhaps, in ways more perplexing, more intense and tragic.

Further Reading

Readers may find the following short list of titles helpful if they wish to read further into the history of Southern racial practices or about the authors represented in this volume.

Indispensable as a starting point is *The Strange Career of Jim Crow,* second revised edition, by C. Vann Woodward. For George Washington Cable, see the biography by Arlin Turner, as well as *The Negro Question: A Selection of Writings in Civil Rights in the South,* by Cable, and edited by Turner. The interested reader will find little pertaining to the life of Thomas U. Dudley, but he can refer to the biographical sketch in *The National Cyclopaedia of American Biography,* III, p. 467, and also to Henry Codman Potter's *Reminiscenses of Bishops and Archbishops,* pp. 163–92. C. Vann Woodward has written a classic biography of Tom Watson; see also by the same author, "Tom Watson and the Negro in Agrarian Politics," *Journal of Southern History,* IV (February, 1938), 14–33. Lewis Harvie Blair was "re-discovered" only a few years ago by two scholars. See *A Southern Prophecy,* C. Vann Woodward's edited version of Blair's *The Prosperity of the South Dependent Upon the Elevation of the Negro,* and Charles E. Wynes, "Lewis Harvie Blair, Virginia Reformer: The Uplift of the Negro and Southern Prosperity," *Virginia Magazine of History and Biography,* LXXII (January, 1964), 3–18. On Andrew Sledd, see Henry Y. Warnock, "Andrew Sledd, Southern Methodists, and the Negro: A Case History," *Journal of Southern History,* XXXI (August, 1965), 65–73. The best account of the "Bassett Affair" is to be found in *Trinity and Duke, 1892–1924,* by Earl W. Porter. On Bassett alone, see the sketch of his life in the *Dictionary of American Biography,* Vol. II, pp. 38–39, and the editorial, "In Memoriam—John Spencer Bassett, *South Atlantic Quarterly,* XXVII (April, 1928), 113–16. Currently the reader will find nothing in print on Quincy Ewing, but there is in press an essay by Charles E. Wynes entitled "The Reverend Quincy Ewing: Southern

Racial Heretic in the Cajun Country." For the story of how Progres-sivism bypassed the Negro, see Dewey W. Grantham, Jr., "The Progressive Movement and the Negro," *South Atlantic Quarterly,* LIV (October, 1955), 461–77. The Woodward essay on Tom Watson and the Negro, the essay on Lewis Blair by Wynes, and the one by Grantham on the Negro and Progressivism may all be found in *The Negro in the South Since 1865: Selected Essays in American Negro History,* edited by Wynes. Finally, to place all the foregoing in con-text, the reader should see Virginius Dabney, *Liberalism in the South.*